Daniel J. Danielsen and the Congo:
Missionary Campaigns and Atrocity Photographs

STUDIES IN BRETHREN HISTORY
Subsidia

Daniel J. Danielsen and the Congo:
Missionary Campaigns and Atrocity Photographs

Óli Jacobsen

BAHN
Brethren Archivists
& Historians Network

2014

Copyright © Óli Jacobsen 2014

First published 2014 by Brethren Archivists and Historians Network

Brethren Archivists and Historians Network
3 Arran Road, Troon, Ayrshire, KA10 6TD

[20 19 18 17 16 15 14 8 7 6 5 4 3 2 1]

The right of Óli Jacobsen (email: olijacobsen@olivant.fo) to be
identified as the Author of this Work has been asserted by him
in accordance with the Copyright, Designs and Patents Act 1988.

British Library Cataloguing in Publication Data
A catalogue record for this book is available from the British Library

ISBN 978-0-9570177-4-0

Typeset, printed, and bound in the Faroe Islands
for Brethren Archivists and Historians Network
by Heildin and Føroyaprent

CONTENTS

LIST OF ILLUSTRATIONS

PREFACE

The only monument to Daniel Jacob Danielsen[1] (1871–1916) is his gravestone in the old cemetery of Tórshavn. It reads *D. J. Danielsen TRÚBOÐI Virkaði i Congo 1901–1903 Ein óræddur hermaður Harrans* [D. J. Danielsen, missionary, Served in the Congo 1901–1903, A fearless soldier of the Lord]. He is remembered locally as one of the very early evangelists of the Brethren movement in the Faroes. He was also the first Faroese to serve as a missionary outside the islands when he worked for the Congo Balolo Mission for two years from 1901 till 1903.[2] Although Danielsen's name is remembered in the Faroe Islands, no research had ever been carried out on the details of his life. I had been writing short biographies of significant Faroese personalities when I decided to fully investigate Danielsen's story. I had no expectation of finding anything of consequence to any history beyond that of the Faroes.

Danielsen evangelised for the Brethren from his return to the Faroes in 1904 till his death in 1916. He travelled widely around the islands over the final twelve years that he spent there, trying to establish and support Brethren assemblies. The Brethren movement became important in the Faroes and Danielsen's involvement at such an early stage makes him a significant figure in Faroese history. Although the more remote communities had been visited by the first British Brethren missionary to the islands, often Danielsen was the first Faroese Brethren worker to approach them. During this period, he wrote regular letters to *Echoes of Service*, a British Brethren missionary magazine, and these letters are republished in this volume. They provide fascinating insight into early twentieth-century Faroese life as well as documenting the early development of a movement which would add so much to Faroese culture.

However, Danielsen had already served in the Congo before this, although it had been for only two years from 1901 till 1903. During this period the Congo Free State had become notorious for its system of forced labour. It is known from Faroese sources that Danielsen had some experience of these events.[3] However, after examining Danielsen's missionary record, I discovered a most unexpected fact. Danielsen assisted Sir Roger Casement (1864–1916), the British consul in the Congo, who undertook in 1903, on behalf of the British government, a survey of the alleged atrocities in the Congo. Danielsen served as captain and engineer on the mission boat Casement had hired to travel in the upper Congo River basin.

The result of my research was a book, *Dollin: Havnarmaðurin, sum broytti heimssøguna* [*Dollin: The Faroese who Changed History in the Congo*].[4] In 2012 I was asked by Neil Dickson, the convenor of the Brethren Archivists and Historians Network (BAHN), to write a summary of the book for its journal *Brethren Historical Review*.[5] While working on that article, and since then, I found more material, which supports the conclusion of the present book that Danielsen was the first missionary to give lantern slide lectures on the atrocities in the Congo. These lectures were an important tool in the work of the Congo Reform Campaign (later the Congo Reform Association [CRA]). The result of the CRA's activity was that Leopold II, the King of Belgium in 1908, had to renounce the Congo as his personal property.

While Danielsen left some writing about his work in the Faroes, he did not write anything about his service in the Congo. His actions and personality have had to be reconstructed from the words of other people. Of course they were not writing a biography of Danielsen, and so often their accounts are frustratingly incomplete or ambivalent for the biographer. One of the main sources for Danielsen's missionary record is the archives of the Congo Balolo Mission (CBM) at New College Library in Edinburgh, which contains two minute books. One of these was kept by the Executive Committee for the mission in London,[6] and the other belonged to the Standing Committee which met in the Congo.[7] The most important information from Executive Committee minutes is an account of an accusation levelled at Danielsen by a disgruntled former mission employee of Danielsen using harsh corporal punishment on his African workers. Frustratingly, although the accusation and initial investigation are well laid out in the minute books, the matter becomes very hazy as it is mentioned over the passing months. Often letters and meetings are referred to which are not copied into the minute books. Presumably these would be more frank about the topic than people evidently were in an executive committee meeting. It is even likely that this was deliberate on the part of the Home Council, as most of its members would know the current state of knowledge about the matter without having it clearly written down. Unfortunately none of the private correspondence between members of the Executive Committee and missionaries seems to be extant. This not only frustrates an effort to know the truth in this particular case, but also excludes us from knowing many other things. For example, often character assessments are made on an individual that came from prior knowledge of him or her that we do not have access to. Interestingly, the Congo Standing

Committee does not mention the matter at all. Its only interest seems to be the day-to-day running of the mission. The monthly magazine of the mission, *Regions Beyond*, is a further source for Danielsen's missionary work, and it contains many contemporary accounts of missionary life. However, as it was for public consumption, it does not contain anything which would tell us more about this complaint, but it is useful for informing us of the duties Danielsen undertook with the CBM in Africa.

Another source for this present work is the Morel papers at London School of Economics.[8] Edmund Dene Morel (1873–1924) was the head of the Congo Reform Association (CRA) and before Danielsen's involvement had already spent several years working to form a publicity campaign to uncover the atrocities known to be taking place in the Congo. He did more than any other person to see that Leopold II was removed from power in the Congo. Morel had a difficult relationship with the Protestant missionaries in the Congo. He relied on them for information in the early days of his campaign, although he felt they were always reluctant to support his cause. As time went on he gave less and less importance to the contributions of anyone working in the mission field towards the work of the CRA. Morel and Danielsen corresponded with each other. However, although there are quite a numbers of letters from Morel to Danielsen extant, only two letters from Danielsen to Morel still exist. That means that the most of the letters from Danielsen are missing.[9]

The third important area available to research was the materials surrounding the Casement Report.[10] The report itself excludes any mention of missionaries who helped with evidence gathering to keep the report impartial. Casement's diary from the time, published posthumously, does make some mention of Danielsen, and these references have been reprinted here.[11] The other material which I have looked at that originated from Casement's period in the Congo was the photographs of atrocity victims. It is my intention to argue in this book that Danielsen is a likely candidate to have taken those photographs.

My research has now come to an end, and therefore I publish this book with the dramatic life story of Danielsen, with special stress on his role in the Congo Campaign. This present work is not an attempt at a full history of the CRA campaign (although a brief account of its work will be found in Chapter 7). A great deal has already been published on the subject; however, none of these works have any mention of Danielsen. With three main sets of sources, all with different reasons to keep Danielsen out of the narrative of the CRA, and in addition with Danielsen not leaving behind any writing himself, it is perhaps no wonder he has not appeared in the official histories of the Congo. He has been a figure completely lost to history. My intention is to give Danielsen the recognition that he deserves. His name was only known for this evangelism in the islands until I started my researches, and even there only by older people. The most important goal of this book has been to bring into the light the role of Danielsen regarding the Congo. That is the reason for writing it in English to reach a wider public. All translations from the Faroese, however, are by myself.

I want to thank all those who have supported and encouraged me in collecting sources and writing this biography. Firstly I wish to thank Neil Dickson. Without his enthusiasm and assistance it is doubtful whether I had continued my research after 2010, and so this history would not have been as complete as it is now. Also a special thanks to his daughter Katie Dickson, who has edited the book and has given advice to improve the manuscript. I thank Quentin Bates for proofreading the document. I have had contact with several Congo historians, Séamas Ó Síocháin, Adam Hochschild, Kevin Grant, Daniel Vangroenweghe and Christina Twomey, and they have all been helpful in commenting on my work.

I am extremely grateful to Dean Pavlakis for generously sharing his researches for his forthcoming book, *British Humanitarianism and the Congo Reform Movement, 1896-1913*. The additional sources he was able to provide and his comments have significantly improved the present work.

Autograph Abp and Anti Slavery International in London have both made helpful contributions, my thanks to all of them.

Óli Jacobsen
16 October 2014
Tórshavn, Faroe Island

PART ONE
CONGO MISSIONARY AND CAMPAIGNER

CHAPTER 1
THE MAKING
OF A MISSIONARY

Daniel Jacob Danielsen was born in Denmark on 25 June 1871 to an un-married mother. Sigrid Frederikke Angelica Danielsen (1841–1922) had left the Faroe Islands in 1865 as a young woman for Copenhagen where she had entered domestic service.[1] Danielsen never knew his father, Ludvig Jørgensen. However, he was baptised in Vor Frue Kirke, the cathedral in Copenhagen, as Ludvig Daniel Jacob. 'Dollin', the name by which he would become known in Faroe, was his pet name and a familiar form of Daniel. He had received this name from his maternal grandfather, also Daniel Danielsen, a carpenter. Fairly soon mother and son returned to the islands, and in 1874 Sigrid married Jákup Jacobsen (1836–1917). She and her husband had five children but only a son, Magnus, survived to adulthood and he later became a prominent Faroese architect, known as Magnus á Kamarinum (1874–1921). Sigrid's eld-est child would not be her only future connection with the Brethren move-ment in the Faroes, as she was also the paternal aunt of Victor Danielsen, who was later a well-known Brethren evangelist in the islands.[2]

Early life
Danielsen grew up in the capital of the Faroe Islands, Tórshavn, which at that time had about 1500 inhabitants. The Faroes are a small group of eighteen in-habited islands lying north-west of Scotland, and on the same line of latitude as southern Norway. The population in the late nineteenth century was about 15,000. Until the nineteenth century, the Faroese economy had been largely based around agriculture and the production of woollen goods. During this century, however, there was a switch to fishing as the main source of income which was much more profitable. The improving economic conditions, along with the introduction of the potato (providing a more stable food crop), led to a rise in population. Tórshavn, and its outlying areas, was the main popu-lation centre, with many other small settlements spread throughout the Far-oes.[3] From 1879 William Gibson Sloan (1838–1914) lived and worked in Tórshavn where he established a Brethren assembly.[4] In all probability, in the small community of Tórshavn, Danielsen would know of Sloan's work before

he left the islands, but there is no evidence that they had any contact with each other at this stage. When Danielsen returned, however, he would continue and extend Sloan's work substantially. None of the organisations he had contact with in Britain were formally connected with the Brethren, but like the Brethren in Scotland, they arose out the same religious movements within transatlantic evangelicalism and had similar ethos and beliefs.

In 1889, at 18, Danielsen went to Scotland to train as an engineer working on ships and steamers. In this period, during the height of the British Empire, there was a great deal of work in this field in Scotland and it was not uncommon for Faroese men to work for a time in Scotland where there were even some communities of Faroese living, especially in Leith, near Edinburgh. He worked mainly for Scottish companies and became something of a globetrotter. We know for sure that he had sailed on ships taking emigrants to America. Danielsen was known to be rather argumentative and impulsive, traits that were to mark him all his life. Nevertheless, his certificates of discharge from the several ships in which he had sailed were marked 'very good', 'both for conduct and acuity'.[5] Later, it would be noted with satisfaction by mission-minded evangelicals, that even in this period of his life he had not been 'under the power of vicious habits.'[6] Although he had a Christian upbringing, he distanced himself from religion of every kind; but in 1898, probably at some point in the spring of that year,[7] at the age of 27, he became radically converted after an open-air service in Glasgow at which he had heard the witness of a Christian worker. After the service Danielsen, and another man from the open-air, went to the meeting hall not far away. In an article describing his conversion he states the question he put to his new companion: 'I asked whether there was a minister there, but he said, that all the children of God were ministers and sons and daughters of God.' This was his first introduction to the lay ethos of late-Victorian revivalism. Some 200 to 300 people were present in the hall, and it was here that Danielsen was converted.[8]

The sequence of events in the eighteen months after his conversion is not entirely clear, due to conflicting accounts of this period.[9] It would appear, however, that he worked with the Seamen's Mission in Glasgow for a time,[10] and it was possibly one of the workers there who later characterised him as a 'thoroughgoing Christian and one who is afraid of nothing in his Master's work'.[11] With a growing desire to be a missionary, he had gone to South Africa for an extended period.[12] It was there he saw an advertisement that changed his life. It was for a Christian marine engineer for the Congo.

Congo missionary

Throughout the nineteenth century, and on into the early decades of the twentieth century, there was a huge missionary movement which sought to spread Christianity to the farthest corners of the world. This impulse was fired in Africa in particular by the full exploration of the interior of that continent. In fact one of the most important early missionary figures, David Livingstone, was also an explorer.[13] From the mid-nineteenth century onwards a movement of 'faith missions' began to establish themselves.[14] One of the most important institutions of the faith mission movement was the East London Institute (ELI), or Harley College, founded in 1873 by the prominent evangelical preacher, Henry Grattan Guinness, and his wife, Fanny Grattan Guinness, both of whom also ran it. Situated in London's east end, the ELI offered vocational training and a wide-ranging educational curriculum, including medical training, to teach cross-cultural ministry skills to potential missionaries. Here students also began to learn to 'live by faith', that is be reliant financially on free-will giving by Christian believers. The school was international, interdenominational and non-proprietry as it allowed its students to join any missionary organisation they liked after leaving.[15]

Although Harley College did not dictate where its students should work, it did have a missionary organisation attached. In 1887 Fanny Grattan Guinness had founded the Livingstone Inland Mission, inspired by Henry Morton Stanley's accounts of his exploration of the Congo River. A year later the first missionaries were sent out to set up mission stations along the lower reaches of the Congo River. Eventually the demands of oversight and funding the mission became too great and responsibility was handed to the American Baptist Missionary Union (ABMU) which was looking for an opportunity to expand.

In 1887 Henry Grattan Guinness and his wife retired, handing the reins of Harley College to their son Dr. Harry Grattan Guinness. He was approached by the Irish Baptist missionary, John McKitterick, who wished to carry out Christian mission further into the interior of the Congo Free State. When it became clear that the American society had, in fact, no intention of expanding, the two men agreed on the creation of a new society to be named the Congo Balolo Mission (CBM), and in August 1889 the first missionaries arrived at their new home. As missions inspired by the Guinnesses and Harley College expanded into new continents, the CBM would become part of the Regions Beyond Missionary Union (RBMU), the name which was increasingly used from 1899 onwards.[16]

After Danielsen had seen the advertisement in South Africa for a Christian engineer, he had evidently returned to Britain, and was interviewed in London by members of the CBM Council and had undergone a thorough medical examination. Two doubts were expressed about his suitability for life as a missionary in the Congo. One was the short period of time since his evangelical conversion, and the other his physical fitness for life in a tropical climate. However, he had the necessary practical skills, and as he had never been ill, he was accepted by the CBM in February 1901, although the doubts over his health was minuted.[17] It is probable that it was after his acceptance that he spent time at Harley College, to prepare for his work as a missionary.[18] It would appear that this was for only about a month, as he sailed for Africa on 11 April 1901.[19]

The Congo Free State

Danielsen would spend two and a half years in the Congo Free State. When he arrived in 1901, that colony had only officially existed for sixteen years. Leopold, at first, commissioned the explorer Henry Morton Stanley and other agents to make treaties with as many local chiefs as possible giving the Belgian king *de facto* sovereignty over as large an area as possible around the Congo River. In 1884-1885, at the Conference of Berlin, the European powers had agreed

Danielson as a young man in national costume.

17

on the rules they would use to carve up Africa into colonies and had set certain standards, seldom adhered to, for governing these colonies. During the Conference, the representatives of Belgium's King Leopold II secured the recognition of the International Congo Association as the government of the Congo, a sleight of hand that had the effect of making that country Leopold's personal domain.

He shored up his claims with a great deal of propaganda about Belgian aims in the territory. Incorporating some of the most popular principles of the day: free trade, freedom of religion, freedom of movement, and the abolition of slavery Leopold promised to create an example of a modern and beneficent colonial power.

It was the commitment to freedom of religion which allowed Protestant missionary groups to operate in the country. Often other European colo-

Harry Grattan Guinness was the leader of The Congo Balolo Mission.

nial powers would only allow missions from the established church of their own country. However in the Congo Free State there were French-speaking Catholics, American Baptists, and Swedish Protestants, as well as the Congo Balolo Mission. The districts that the CBM operated in were on the upper Congo and very remote. They were in the heart of rubber growing districts. Rubber was a natural by-product of red rubber trees. To collect the rubber the trees had to be 'tapped' and the Congo Free State imposed a system of forced labour on local Africans to collect it. The brutal nature of this system would eventually be exposed in such a manner that Leopold would be forced to pass the territory to the Belgian state.

Missionaries played a dual role in the controversies surrounding the Congo Free State. In the first instance King Leopold courted the Protestant missionaries and recognised that they could be of use to him in many ways. Their presence alone lent a certain legitimacy to the humanitarian rhetoric surrounding King Leopold's administration. In the nineteenth century freedom of religion was a modern principle still not observed universally. The free movement of Protestant missionaries in a colony ruled by a Roman Catholic monarch looked impressive, especially to the largely Protestant British public. Leopold also rewarded specific acts which were useful to him. Edward Ruskin was a missionary with the CBM from 1894. He took a special interest in Lomongo, one of the two languages spoken locally in the region. Within his lifetime Ruskin printed a translation of the New Testament into Lomongo in 1908 and the entire Bible in 1930. His wife, Lily, was also engaged in the translation as, she too, was a specialist in the language, and eventually wrote a fictionalised account of the Congo atrocities in *Bokwala*

Leopold II, King of the Belgians.

(1909 – see Appendix 2). Ruskin was recognised for this work by Leopold as his work could also prove useful to the state.[20] The most sophisticated use that Leopold made of the missionaries was as a counter to the increasing criticism of his regime in the Congo. The Commission for the Protection of the Natives was launched by Leopold with both Catholic and Protestant missionaries sitting on it.[21] It proved largely ineffective in investigating the problems faced by Congolese peoples; however, this provided Leopold with the credibility he required.

E. D. Morel, who will be a major figure in Danielsen's story (see chapter 3), spent many years running a campaign against the atrocities being committed in the Congo Free State.

Eventually the publicity he generated would prompt the British government to commission the Casement report.

This relates to the second role that missionaries fulfilled in the Congo. As actors independent of Belgian control in rubber growing districts, missionaries were often the source of many criticisms of Leopold's regime. In fact the Commission for the Protection of the Natives was launched in reaction to specific claims made by Edvard Sjöblom, a Swedish missionary working in the Congo with the American Baptist Mission.[22] This second role could prove uncomfortable for missionaries. Working in remote locations, good relations with state officials were to be encouraged, but, on the other hand, the missionaries were sufficiently independent that they could get papers out of the country without facing Belgian censorship. The somewhat reluctant stance that Protestant missionaries took would eventually lead Morel to discount their role in the Congo Reform Movement. However, as will be seen later, that role was significant.

The collection of rubber in the Congo. The cover of the book The Eyes of Another Race.

The Congo Balolo Mission

Danielsen was stationed at Bonginda, roughly a thousand miles up the Congo River, where he arrived in mid-July 1901.[23] He was assigned to the SS *Pioneer*, a recent gift from the Irish YMCAs, as captain and engineer. He was the sole European in the crew, which would also have included local men who worked as woodcutters and deckhands. The work of the CBM at that time was described in the mission's magazine, *Regions Beyond*:

> The Congo Balolo Mission has six stations on the Upper Congo – at Leopoldville, Lolanga, Bonginda, Bonbandanga and Baringa. During the last 15 years over One Hundred Missionaries have been sent out, of whom thirty have died. Thirty two

As the rubber trees were drained, it became necessary to climb higher to reach the rubber.

are now in the field. The mission is served by two steamers, the SS *Pioneer* and the SS *Livingstone* and had established a printing press in Bonbandanga. Its workers have reduced two native languages – Eleko and Lomongo – to writing, and a large amount of translation work, including the greater part of the New Testament has been accomplished in the latter. Over two thousand children are taught in its day schools and a large amount of itinerant work is done in the villages adjoining the stations. During 1903 the work has been specially promising and shows every sign of becoming a power amongst the Congo people.[24]

Although only in the Congo for just over two years, we know quite a lot of Danielsen's work as a missionary and as an engineer. In *Regions Beyond* can be found notes about Danielsen written by Revd William Douglas Armstrong, the leader of the mission in Bonginda, and there was also a mission book

THE APPEAL.

"IN THE NAME OF ALMIGHTY GOD.—All the Powers exercising sovereign rights, or having influence in the said territories undertake to watch over the preservation of the native races, and the amelioration of the moral and material conditions of their existence."

Article VI. The Act of Berlin, 1885.

Cartoon printed in Regions Beyond in 1908. Note the caption beneath it holding Leopold to the principles he had initially used to convince the public of his good intentions in the Congo.

Harley House, Bow, London E. The headquarters of The Regions Beyond Missionary Union.

kept in the Congo in which details of his time can be seen. Danielsen quickly became a trusted member of the engineering department. The CBM minutes recorded with satisfaction that

> Letters received indicate that the two Engineers sent out, Danielson and Wallbaum, were in every sense satisfactory. The *Pioneer* is running under the charge of Mr. Danielson, whose Mr. Gilchrist describes as a most capable man, extremely tidy in everything. Mr. Danielson reports that he finds the *Pioneer* a good little craft and with care will last some years yet although she will not stand any rushing about or heavy storms.[25]

By June 1902 *Regions Beyond* was reporting, 'Our Danish Brother [*sic*] is proving himself a real acquisition. One missionary writes: "He makes things most comfortable for his passengers. We are very thankful for him. The *Pioneer* quite outdoes her old self in his hands."'[26] Danielsen was often present at meetings of the Standing Committee, the mission field committee which met in the Congo, probably partly due to the fact that he would have been needed to bring other members to the meeting place. In May 1902, when the previous head of the engineering department retired, Danielsen was made temporary head of engineering.[27] Obviously he was an able engineer as well as a good manager of people.

The most important project which Danielsen was tasked with in his time as head engineer was the re-assembly of the SS *Livingstone* in the Congo. The ship was first built in England and afterwards brought to the Congo in sections. A number of problems relating to the new ship were found, and so it was proposed that a slip be constructed in Bonginda to make it possible to take the vessel ashore. The project was eventually successfully completed. In the Executive Committee minutes for October 1902 this is included:

> A resolution was proposed... unanimously carried, that the Council have heard with infinite pleasure and thankfulness of the rapid re-construction and satisfac-

The village of Bonginda.

tory trial trips of the *Livingstone* and wish to record their appreciation of the splendid work performed in this connection by the Engineers and their staff and thanks to all who had had any share in this work.[28]

Mission ships were piloted by skilled mission men, but most of the labour on board was provided by local Congolese people. Congolese workers spent their nights sleeping on the river banks and were expected to collect enough wood in the mornings to run the steamer for that day. This task seems to have caused a great deal of tension between workers and mission engineers. Alice Harris, a CBM missionary at Baringa, has this account of a trip on the *Pioneer*:

> Our trip on the *Pioneer* has been somewhat slow, owing to constant palavers over "wood cutting."[29] There are few men on board who work splendidly, always obtaining their quantity of wood, no matters how the others fail. If only it was

The Congo Balolo Mission station at Bonginda.

> possible to man the Steamers with Christian men what enormous amount of troubles might be saved! There are two Christians among the crew who set a splendid example. They have their wives on board and we often enjoy with [*sic*] the latter on shore, while the wood cutters are at work.[30]

As well as his duties as an engineer, Danielsen was particularly keen to engage in missionary work. This may have made him a little unusual amongst his colleagues. In November 1901 Armstrong noted that Danielsen 'looks forward to preaching the Gospel as soon as he shall have acquired the language.'[31] This process was obviously completed by 1903 when Armstrong writes:

July 1903:
The Christian men often go down on Sundays and hold meetings, so that they get three services a week. The itinerant work suffers somewhat from the fact that I am the only one able to undertake it. However, when the engineers are here, Mr. Danielson kindly takes the morning service week about, and leave me free to make excursions. I have in this way been able to go out three times lately.[32]

According to Faroese sources, Danielsen was well known for his sense of humour,[33] and this characteristic was a great help in various disputes among the locals. The people looked to the missionary for protection and made demands on his wisdom. The missionary was expected to settle quarrels and disagreements.

In reading missionary material from the period, it emerges that one of their main preoccupations was fighting against the perceived pagan nature of African society. This was often best expressed in conflict with native shamans, the local witch-doctors:

> The witch-doctors, as a class, used all their arts to drive us out of the country. They seemed to know that if once the people accepted our message, their livelihood would be gone. If one of our party was ill, the witch-doctor gave out that

Danielsen was the skipper and engineer of the old mission boat Pioneer.

D. J. DANIELSON.

Daniel J. Danielsen

he had caused the illness, and the malign influence these wicked men exercised over the others was so great that they believed entirely in all their vile impostures, and feared to offend them.[34]

One incident is recorded where Danielsen came into contact with a local witch-doctor. A servant of Danielsen's was ill and close to death. It was revealed that the witch doctor in the village was thought to have caused the sickness. Danielsen went to the witch doctor and demanded that he end his magic. Initially the witch-doctor refused to do so, and therefore Danielsen threatened to report the case to the Belgian authorities, which had banned such activity. The threat had the desired effect and the witch doctor took away bird claws and similar material. It was all burnt on a fire, and the sick man recovered.[35]

A native shaman.

A Day on the "Pioneer."

Article from Regions Beyond in 1902.

THOUGH our new steamer, the *Livingstone*, should, please GOD, be afloat by this time, we must not forget the old *Pioneer*. Mr. Danielson, the Danish brother who has gone out to take charge of her, gives a good account of her. Though by herself she is hopelessly inadequate to the needs of our work, Mr. Danielson says after a good deal of patching up he finds her a good little craft, which with good care will last us some years yet; though of course she will not stand any knocking about. He adds:—

"Perhaps it will interest you to know how I spend a day in the *Pioneer*. I rise at 3.30 a.m., and tell the men to bring on board the

wood they have cut overnight, and order the firemen to get steam up. When the wood is on board and the steam rising, I call all the men and boys—forty-five in all—forward in front of the cabin, and have service: two hymns and a few prayers. Service finished, we loose the ship, and proceed on our day's run at 5.30.

"How beautiful to be on this river on a good morning, just as the sun comes over the horizon! Truly we see the wonderful works of our GOD.

"After flushing the deck, we have breakfast at 7.30, and dinner at 11.30, then midday rest. But this last is for the passengers only, the skipper has to keep his eyes open, looking ahead so as to avoid rocks and sandbanks, for they are plentiful. However, accidents may happen to the most careful.

"Our last meal we take at 5.30 p.m., when we generally stop for the night to cut wood for the next day's journey. Then the engineer, or skipper as you may call him, is glad to get to his cabin to praise the LORD for a good day's run, and to get rest, though often that rest is very broken."

CHAPTER 2
SERIOUS ACCUSATIONS

In December 1901 Mr. Sawyers, a carpenter in the employ of the CBM, was fired for incompetence. In November 1902 Sawyers appeared before the Home Council of the CBM and complained that he had not been given a chance to speak in his own defence. He then made a series of allegations which were so serious in nature that Dr. Grattan Guinness called a session the next day to hear the full charges. They involved the use of a chicotte, a hippopotamus-hide, four-strip whip. This is the full recorded statement from the minute books:

A palaver; a conference held to settle disputes.

Mr. Sawyers stated to the Council that he had resided for five weeks at Bonginda with Mr. Clarke on his journey down country. He left Baringa on 8th August and was at Bonginda the last two weeks in August and the whole of September.

During the whole of that period Mr. Danielson used the chicotte, and on the steamer the latter was a daily occurrence when the men were flogged every morning if they had not brought in a certain quantity of wood. That the men were laid on the ground and received twenty five blows each.

The chicotte used a thong with four tails plaited together.

Mr. Danielson put men and women in the stocks; the women because their husbands or friends did not bring sufficient wood. Mr. Sawyers says he saw more than once men and women in the stocks during his stay at Bonginda. He had never seen the stocks used elsewhere than at Bonginda.

Mr. Sawyers was asked whether he was aware of any other person in the Mission striking a native with the chicotte. He answered at first in the negative but subsequently said that Mr. Wallbaum had not only seen Mr. Danielson do it but that Mr. Wallbaum had done it himself several times. Sawyers saw him do it "more than seven times but not a dozen".

He said that Mr. Armstrong, Mr. Gilchrist and other members of the Mission were aware of these practises.

Mr. Sawyers had heard (by report only) that Mr. Ellery had flogged a woman at Ikau and also her little girls.

Although the natives were stupid and had to be shown practically every detail of work, they had never been troublesome to Mr. Sawyers personally in connection with the carpentering department. He considered they work fairly well.

He never saw Mr. Gilchrist use the chicotte while he was Captain of the steamer.

Mr. Sawyers also stated that when staying at Bonginda Mr. Armstrong went out to one of the villages to have a service.

When he came back to the station he told Mr. Clark and Mr. Sawyers that the people would not come out willingly to listen and that he had taken their pots and pans and other goods and thrown them into the river.

On another occasion Mr. Armstrong went out to secure some fowls. But as the supply was finished in the near town the people had to go far off into another town to get some. As they did not bring any Mr. Armstrong shot six of their fowls and brought them to Bonginda station. He made no payment whatever for them. He made no secret of it and told Mr. Clarke what he had done.

There is very little information available about Sawyers. We know with certainty that he came from Jamaica, as the mission gave him passage back to there, his place of origin, and he has tentatively been identified as Terence B. Sawyers from St. Ann in Jamaica.[1] As one of two Afro-Caribbean men in an otherwise all-white mission, Sawyers' place was unusual and difficult. It upset the social order which missionaries in the Congo were unthinkingly carrying out. Accepting a black man as an equal and a colleague would have been difficult for people living out the racist ideologies of the time.

Sawyers' race could explain both the lack of support for him and his claims from his colleagues and his desire to complain in the first place. He would not have been as likely to be susceptible to dominant ideologies. George Washington Williams provides an example of the response which an African American had to events in the Congo. Williams visited the Congo in 1890. His outrage at what he saw taking place there led him to write that what was happening in the Congo Free State amounted to 'crimes against humanity'.[2] He produced various letters and pamphlets detailing the grave nature of what he had seen happening in the Congo Free State. Both men came from communities which had recent experience of slavery; the practice was abolished in Jamaica in 1834 and in the US in 1865. Williams' position clearly made a difference to how he viewed events he witnessed in the Congo; it is possible that the same was true of Sawyers.

The story about Armstrong which comes at the end of the statement was eventually confirmed by others, as the CBM minutes note. The confiscation of goods was seen as an ethical and entirely legitimate alternative for missionaries as opposed to human hostage-taking practised by the State. Both of these actions were aimed at gaining the cooperation of local Africans to complete work on others' behalf. While a simplistic identification must be avoided between colonialism and mission, missionaries often shadowed the behaviour of the colonial state towards local Africans. Although the element of personal violence was removed, missionaries still expected locals to provide them with goods and services free of charge.

Questions and answers

On the 4th December 1902 any missionary home from the Congo on furlough was called before the Council to give evidence on this matter. The conference was opened with prayer after which Dr. Guinness briefly stated the object of the gathering. He mentioned that in the report of the first united conference of missionaries held the previous January at Leopoldville there was in his opinion one grave omission from the discussion – the relation of the Missionaries in connection with the system of labour in Congo. The position of the CBM had been clearly indicated in the revised 'Principles and Practice', which had now been printed. The question of corporal punishment (which had formed the subject of long and earnest discussions at the meetings of the Home Council) had been dealt with Clause 17 (c) reading as follows:

The indiscriminate use of corporal punishment is absolutely forbidden. Light forms of such punishment may be occasionally necessary, but should be employed with discretion and preferable after consultation with a fellow missionary.

Serious flogging must in no case resorted so, as being totally opposed to the Spirit of Christ and the principles of the Mission.

Dr. Guinness then put a series of questions, to each of the missionaries present:

Question 1:

Have you ever used chicotte for purposes of corporal punishment?

Answers:

All replied in the negative, save Mr. Wilkes, who said he had used it once at Skaw in 1897 during the time of the revolts against The India Rubber Traffic around Skaw, when attacked by the natives from the back. That was not a matter of labour, and was quite exceptional.

Question 2:

Have you seen the chicotte employed by any other member of the Mission?

Answers:

Messrs. Ruskin, Bowen and Gamman replied in the negative and Mr. Wilkes referred to the instance in answer 1.

Mr. Black replied that he had not exactly seen in done but was within a few yards when it was done.

Question 3:

Have any of you got absolutely reliable information that causes you to believe that any other member of the Mission has used the chicotte?

Answers:

Mrs. Ruskin: It has been used in the past. It was used on the *Pioneer* in Mr. McGregor's time. I do not know of any other case for certain.

Mr. Ruskin: I have been given to understand Mr. Harris used it.

Mr. Gamman: I have never used it or seen Mr. Ellery use it. I was two years on Skaw station. I have known workmen and boys be treated with a stick.

Mr. Bowen: I have only known of it by hearsay. Harris spoke to me about it being done at Skaw. He thought our natives at Bongandanga were better.

Mr. Black: I have only heard that a Captain did it for Ellery. Mr. Danielson certainly has used it. He had also had natives chicotted by the state men after reporting to the Judge at Leopoldville.

Mr. Wilkes: The natives have told me that Mr. Ellery used it.

Algernon and Lily Ruskin, William Wilkes, Mr. Bowen and H. G. Gamman were all missionaries; however, Mr. Black was an engineer. It is interesting to note the differences in his replies. Although shy of admitting any direct knowledge ('Mr. Black replied that he had not exactly seen in done but was within a few yards when it was done'), he admits to knowing that both Danielsen and another Captain had both used the chicotte. Lily Ruskin also admits that she knew Mr. McGregor had used it when he piloted the *Pioneer* (now Danielsen's boat). Life on board ship in the early twentieth century was harsh. Many of the engineers would have experienced strict discipline in their working lives. Black would have had a more detailed knowledge of how discipline was kept on mission steamers and so his words should be given extra consideration.

The names of the missionaries William Wilkes, John Harris, and John Ellery also come up with regard to the chicotte. This may have to do with the way that rumours grew up in isolated mission posts. There was so much violence being committed in the Congo that some would eventually attach itself to the missionaries themselves. However, some stories were more pernicious than others and the one about Ellery seems to have caused a great deal of comment. We cannot know that the statements are full accounts of what was said in this session but they hardly exonerate missionaries in the field from involvement with the harsher forms of corporal punishment.

Mr. Black.

Mr. H. Wallbaum.

Question 4:
Have anyone heard of Mr. Gilchrist using the chicotte or sending people to be flogged by the State?
Answers in the negative from all
It was mentioned that a State man who had no authority to do it gave a chicotte to Danielson. A few State Captains only have permission to administer corporal punishment.

Dr. Guinness then mentioned the accusation made by Mr. Sawyers against Mr. Armstrong and asked whether the other members of the Mission knew anything about the matter.

Mr. Black said he had known Armstrong to take workmen and boys and go into the villages and search their houses of the natives and brought the property on to the Mission until the fowls were brought. That was done as a kind of hostage.

Mr. Gamman said that these villages were set apart for this very purpose, and that they had consequently did not work rubber…

Mr. Harben said that he had expostulated when fowls were not brought, but went without. He had spoken to the Director of the Rubber Co. on the matter who had advised. The chief being put into the State prison for a week.

Question 5

Has any known of any person in our Mission putting natives into prison i.e. has a prison been kept on any Stations?

Answers:

Mr. Black said that at Lulanga a place was kept which was used as a prison and he had known people kept there under Mr. Gilchrist's order.

Mr. Armstrong had asked him to take a man down to Coquilhatville on account of his not having brought in fresh food, but he (Black) has purposely allowed him to escape.

The result of the foregoing enquiries is that no one has seen any abuse of power on the part of any brother on our Stations, except Mr. Black.

Mr. Sawyers was then called and made the following statement in reply to questions put to him:

When I came down in the *Livingstone* from Bonginda to the Pool, during the nine days I was on board. Danielson used the chicotte six days out of nine. I saw it employed every week day.

Sometimes 9 men sometimes 5, sometimes 12 men were flogged at a time, receiving as many as 25 blows each. Mr. Danielson himself administrates them.

I did not expostulate with him. I told nobody of this, except this council.

While I was staying at Bonginda I saw two of the wives of the Bonginda workmen and one woman from a town chicotted. I believe Mr. Armstrong knows of this although I cannot say positively. The women were made to lie down on the ground – not held by a man – and Danielson chicotted them. I saw this with my own eyes. It took place near the workshop – about 100 yards from Mr. Armstrong's House.

Mr. Sawyers also repeated his statement about Mr. Armstrong shooting fowls. He said that the people are supposed to bring in fowls once a week, but at Bonginda the fowls are very scarce, so they have to go some distance to get them.

With regard to the accusations against Mr. Ellery of flogging girls. Mr. Sawyers said that Mr. James who was an eye witness, told him of the occurrence.

It was stated by the other missionaries that the two girls referred to were now either Church Members or… at Skaw Station.

Mr. Sawyers admitted that he had used a stick on his personal boy, but never a chicotte.

He said he had also seen Mr. Wallbaum chicotte men several times at Bonginda Station not more than two at a time. He had never seen Wallbaum chicotte a woman.

Mr. Sawyers on retiring was warned that he must never again allude to the matters above referred to.

Sawyers' description of the chicotte and its use matches contemporary accounts of how the State punished its prisoners. At this stage Sawyers repeats his accusations against Wallbaum, another engineer, of using the chicotte. On the subject of Wallbaum, Sawyers changes his mind several times. In his first statement he at first denies anyone other than Danielsen ever used the chicotte and then accuses Wallbaum of using it several times. Of course that could have been to do with the way the question was being put each time. The questions are not recorded.

Mr. Black also retired at this stage and the Council then considered with the Missionaries his relationship to the Mission.

They all expressed their appreciations of Mr. Black's skill as an Engineer and particularly his work in connection of the *Livingstone*. His only fault was that he had a most unfortunate way of rubbing everyone up the wrong way. The missionaries were unanimous that it would be well to retain Mr. Black's services suggesting that he should have a period of training in the College, which would probably rub up some of the rough corners.

On the motion of Mr. Irvine seconded by Mr. Elasham it was unanimously decided that Dr. Guinness should have another interview with Mr. Black and if he were willing, arrangements were to be made for his entering the college after Christmas.

While missionaries were mainly from a middle-class background, engineers would be more likely to be from a different class and even country. Sawyers, Black, and Danielsen himself, are all sent out to the Congo as workers and therefore stand slightly apart from the missionaries. The similarities in the complaints made against them are noticeable. It is often phrased as above:

'he had a most unfortunate way of rubbing everyone up the wrong way'. The subtle workings of the class system are evident here as they are elsewhere in these interactions.

Sawyers and Black suffer a fate common to many whistle-blowers in other organisations. Instead of having the matter fully investigated, both were quietly silenced, and punished for making accusations in the first place.

The general feeling of the Council at the close of the discussion as expressed by Mr. Irvine was that there has been no serious abuse of power on the part of any of the Missionaries (with the sole exception of Mr. Danielson) and that it was evidently necessary and wise at certain to exercise discipline from a parental standpoint – which was altogether different from the course adopted from the traders and the State.

The council unanimously decided that a letter should be sent to the Field Committee with reference to the matters discussed at this Conference and urging that steps to be taken to prevent recurrence of the use of the chicotte. A communication was also to be sent to Mr. Danielson on the subject.

Also in that connection with the accusation against Mr. Armstrong the Council urge that the greatest care be taken that the limits of propriety are not exceeded.[3]

The S.S. Livingstone, *the principal boat of the Congo Balolo Mission.*

Up until this point a fairly clear record of events exists, but as the months went on things become murkier. A great deal of communication must have taken place which was not put on record. Although the matter was promptly investigated in London, no reply had been received by March:

> It being quite evident that Mr. Danielson has violated the rules of the Mission his immediate recall was suggested. But after some consideration it was agreed that the matter should stand over until an answer to Dr. Guinness' letter has been received from the Field Committee.[4]

Terence B. Sawyers from Jamaica, probably the Mr Sawyers from Jamaica who worked for the CBM.

At the council meeting 28 May 1903 'the secretary reported that Mr. Black… had retired from the Mission, and that Mr. Danielson had been recalled from the field.'[5] Matters were apparently progressing at a much quicker rate in London than in the Congo. Eventually the Standing Committee provided their response to the allegations:

Present: Mr. Ellery (Chairman), Mr. Gilchrist, Mr. Jeffrey, Mr. Whiteside, Mr. Wallbaum, Mr. Armstrong (Secretary)

Item 14. Mr. Danielson's dismissal by the Home Council

Mr. Wilke's letter of April 9th was read in which he stated that a letter which had been received from one of our member, had been read by the Council, and as a result they unanimously recommended Mr. Danielson's recall from the field, and that six months' notice had been given him. After much discussion, the following minute was passed:

Proposed by Mr. Jeffrey and seconded by Mr. Armstrong that as Mr. Danielson in his letter, which has been sent to us here in Committee, clears himself of the charges which were brought against him by Messrs Sawyers and Black, we do not consider that the facts stated in Gilchrist's letter form a sufficient ground for the action of the home council in dismissing him. (Carried by five votes.)

A report of Mr. Danielson's work is embodied in the accompanying letter to be sent to the Home Council:

Some of the more important items of Mr. Danielson's work during the last two years are as follows:

1. Repairing the hull of the *Pioneer* and pulling gin plates in the forward part of the ship.
2. Rebuilding the boiler.
3. From January to the middle of June he was occupied in making three trips to the Pool, Baringa, and Bongandanga, without accident or touching either sandbanks or rocks. The *Livingstone* then came up and he was occupied at stopping the leakages, the stern wheel was covered in and the ship generally overhauled. Then followed two trips to the Pool and up river without touching rocks or sandbanks. The slip was then commenced, and he got in about 2,000 feet of log and squared it up for the slipway. The digging of the slip has under his superintendence and the pulling down of half the rails. Mr. Danielson is orderly, painstaking, and thorough in all his work and possesses untiring energy. I think I may safely say that no one has worked harder than he, and his has never spared himself. He kept good discipline, and the men work well under him. When he is in charge of the steamer he looks well after the comfort of the passengers and the boat is kept very clean. I may add that we have remarked no spiritual declension in him whilst he has been on the Congo. He frequently helps in the morning services at Bonginda and he has made more effort to acquire the language than any Engineer since Morroy.[6]

Sawyers' claims are hard to evaluate at this distance. It could be that his race elicited the responses he got both from the missionaries in the field and the members of the home council, but there is no evidence to support this other than his (assumed) ethnicity.

Black's evidence, when placed alongside Sawyers', hardly makes the picture clearer. We could also presume that there was some level of truth to accusations about the chicotte being used infrequently on mission steamers. These are repeated often enough to seem authentic. However the magnitude of the accusations against Danielsen are so out of character when compared to any other assessment of him that they seem unlikely. Although others would offer their thoughts and opinions on Danielsen no one repeats the kind of accusations which Sawyers makes here.

After the receipt of the standing committees' letter Guinness made this statement:

> Dr. Harry [Grattan Guinness] explained to the council that whereas Mr. Danielson had been released from the Field because of certain charges made against him by private individuals and these charges having been proved false or gross exaggerations this recall had been withdrawn.[7]

After Danielsen's recall was withdrawn, the matter was considered closed. But as Danielsen had been coming down river on his way home, his life had taken an unexpected turn. He had been asked to sail up the Congo River for what would prove to be his final time. He had decided to do so, this time on an older boat, the SS *Henry Reed*. He was to escort to the Upper Congo the British consul for eastern Congo, Roger Casement.[8]

CHAPTER 3
CASEMENT'S COMPANION

George Edmond Pierre Achille Morel-de-Ville, known by the *nom de plume* E. D. Morel, served with the Elder Dempster Shipping Company, British shipping agents with that served West Africa and that had contracts in the Congo Free State. Morel had joined the company as a clerk and worked his way up to become head of the Congo department. During this period Morel began writing on West African affairs for various British newspapers. After

Photo by]   [*Russell & Sons.*
MR. E. D. MOREL.

" Our clients are the millions of **defenceless men, women and children,** whose torture and destruction has been proceeding steadily for fourteen long years. . . . In the name of humanity, of common decency, for honour's sake, if for no other cause, will not the Anglo-Saxon race make up their minds to handle this **monstrous outrage** resolutely, and so point a way and set an example which others would then be compelled to follow ? "

E. D. MOREL.

George Edmond Pierre Achille Morel-de-Ville known as E. D. Morel.

he had secured a job with the Elder Dempster Shipping Company, he had set about reading everything he could about West Africa to make himself an expert on the subject.[1] Morel began to observe that the ships coming from the Congo imported valuables such as ivory and rubber but they only carried out weapons and luxury items. The imbalance in trade troubled the young Morel, and the more he looked into the situation in the Congo, the clearer it became to him that events of great importance were in motion there, but that the public in Europe generally, and Britain particularly, was totally ignorant of them. Morel initially approached his boss at Elder Dempster with his conclusions. However, when he was turned away by him, Morel quit his job and began writing full-time, first for the *West Africa*, and then later launching his own newspaper the *West African Mail*.[2]

Morel began a sustained writing campaign attacking the governance of the Congo Free State. He had sources within the Belgian administration who fed him information. He also was in contact with British, American and Scandinavian missionaries who were working in the region.[3] Morel's attacks were well publicised and sustained. When the Belgians tried to discredit his claims Morel could often provide documentary evidence to prove them.[4] The success of his campaigning led to important people in British society becoming interested in the issue and taking it up in Parliament. In 1903 Morel and his allies succeeded in having the issue debated in the House of Commons. The important result of the debate was that the British consul in the area was sent to investigate affairs in the Congo. Roger Casement's report would prove a turning point in the whole campaign.

Danielsen meets Casement

The Conference of Berlin of 1884–5, which had first recognised Leopold's colony, had put a burden on the signatory states to oversee that the administration was truly in keeping with its expressed 'humanitarian' principles. The

Roger Casement.

constant trickle of information about the Congo Free State that had triggered the parliamentary debate of 1903 in the UK, led the British government to send a consul to the Congo to report on conditions on the ground there.

Roger Casement had been the British consul based in Boma since 1900. A native of Dublin, he had been working in sub-Saharan Africa for some time before he began working for the British government. Casement had already spent some time ten years earlier working in the districts of the Congo Free State that he would now be investigating. He was in many ways ideal for the job. He was very much alive to the kinds of evidence which would be persuasive to the British government, and therefore he does not simply note that villages in proximity to Belgian stations were required to provide food-stuffs. He gives the exact type of food and the weight expected to be produced, as well as any payment in kind given for this work. This sort of exactitude not only gave his report an obvious authority, it also made it extremely difficult for the Belgian government to refute any of its specific points.

Casement was an unusual man to find working for the British government in this period. His obvious sympathy for the peoples of the Congo and his determination to do something for them was not in keeping with the imperialist attitudes prevalent at the time. One of his first actions on returning to

The ABMU steamer S.S. Henry Reed, used by Roger Casement on his expedition. Danielson was the skipper and engineer on board.

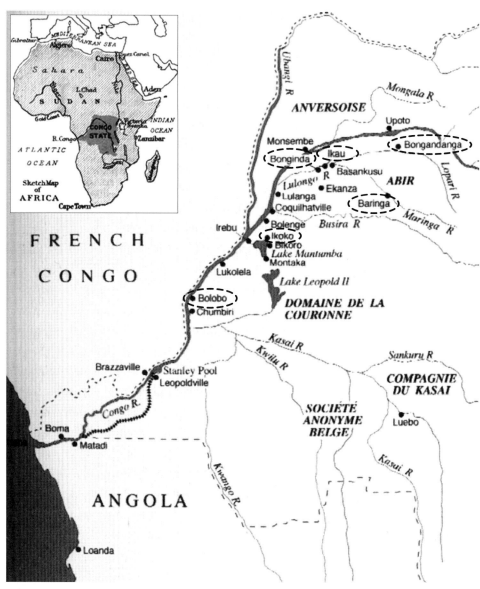

Map of Congo Free State (portion)

The Congo river and its tributaries. Danielsen was hired as engineer on Henry Reed *in Bolobo. They sailed up to Bongandango, and then back to Leopoldville.*

Map: Séamas O Siocháin.

The distances were as follows:

Leopoldville, about 360 miles from the coast. Lolanga, upper Congo, about 960 miles inland. Bonginda, river Lolongo, about 1.000 miles inland. Ikau, river Lolongo, about 1080 miles inland. Bongandanga, river Lopori, about 1210 miles inland. Baringa, river Maringa, about 1200 miles inland.

Britain was to meet with E. D. Morel and encourage him to create the Congo Reform Association. For many years he had been sending reports to the Foreign Office detailing the situation in West Africa. Now that an opportunity had presented itself to do something about the situation, he had jumped at the chance.

Unsurprisingly the Belgian authorities were not entirely accommodating of Casement's aims. It soon became clear that if he wanted to travel freely in the colony, he would need to find some independent means of travel. At this point the Protestant English-speaking missionaries became important allies. Casement had already established links with some missionaries. He had worked for the Baptist Missionary Society in a lay capacity.[5] Casement had

Illustration of Sentries attacking the village of Bolime in Central Congo. Printed from The Graphic *(January, 1906).*

tried while at Brazzaville, French Congo, in June to charter a small steam launch from one of the French firms there but the terms asked were altogether disproportionate. It had been FF3000 per month for the hire of the vessel alone, with several other charges and, in the event of loss, the entire cost of her full value. Instead, in July 1903, he hired a steamer, the SS *Henry Reed*, from the American Baptist Missionary Union, which in the event would only cost about £53, with further minor expenses in pay for African members of the crew.[6] The ship, however, would need an engineer, and after a meeting on 17 July Danielsen agreed to take on the job. That day Casement wrote in his diary: 'Got Danielson for Engineer of "Reed".'[7]

On his survey Casement spoke to as many people as he came across about conditions in the Congo Free State. He spoke with soldiers, state officials, doctors and missionaries. He also talked to the African people he met. However, Casement could not speak any local languages. He was therefore reliant for most of his trip on Danielsen to act as an interpreter for him. In *The Eyes of Another Race* (2003), which reprints Casement's report and publishes his diary for 1903, this dramatic journey has been described.[8] It is evident from Casement's diaries and report that Danielsen assisted him with his survey.[9]

Congo survey

The map on page 44 shows the route taken by the consul's party and where they stopped and visited. Casement and Danielsen were the only white men on the boat. As on the CBM boats, there were a number of locals whose task was to cut wood as fuel for the engine. Sailing on the Congo on an elderly boat was not straightforward, and among the incidents Danielsen would deal with were grounding on a sandbank and a boiler tube bursting.[10]

Throughout July, Casement and his party would thoroughly explore the rubber growing districts. The system of forced labour in practice there had many brutal aspects. The most infamous would become the cutting-off of hands by *Force Publique* soldiers. An account taken from the Casement Report, given by a Belgian official who was being invalided home when Casement met him, states:

Each time the corporal goes out to get rubber cartridges are given to him. He must bring back all not used; and for every one used he must bring back a right hand.' M.P. [Congo Free State official whose name was redacted in the report] told me that sometimes they shot a cartridge at an animal in hunting; they then cut off a hand from a living man. As to the extent to which this is carried on, he informed me that in six months they, the State, on the Momboyo River, had

Mola Ekulite and Yoka, taken at the ABMU mission station in Ikoko.

used 6000 cartridges, which means that 6000 people are killed or mutilated. It means more than 6000, for the people have told me repeatedly that the soldiers kill children with the butt of their guns.[11]

Quickly a routine was established for the trip: Casement would make stops along his route and walk into the bush, visiting as many villages and talking to as many people as he was able. As translator Danielsen would be of central importance to these ventures. On the 25th of July Casement visited the BMS station at Lukoela where John Whitehead, one of the missionaries, criticized both the excessively heavy labour taxation and the ill treatment of African witnesses who had been called upon to establish cases of cruelty on the part of the State agents. He explained that the persecution of African witnesses made missionaries hesitant to lodge complaints.[12]

Four days later Casement was at Lake Mantumba where he visited a village called Ikoko. The first photographs which we can trace from the journey were taken here of Mola Ekulite and Yoka, two boys who had had their hands cut off. These photographs were of great importance in the following public campaign in Britain against the Congo Free State. It would mark the first time an account of an atrocity could be illustrated so clearly to the public. The photographs themselves were cleverly taken. A white sarong-like cloth worn on the victim's lower body and legs served two purposes: firstly it covered the nakedness that might not be readily acceptable to a Victorian British audience, and secondly it provided a stark visual contrast against which to display the severed limb clearly.

In Ikoko Casement noted a phenomenon which would become familiar on his travels. While Ikoko once had a population of between four or five thousand it was now home to only 600 people.[13] Much of the population had fled from

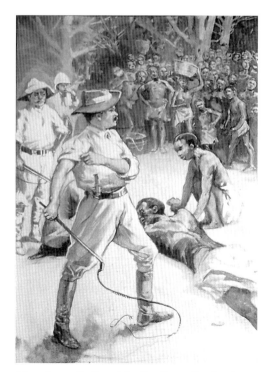

Flogging with the chicotte. From the book Bokwala.

Lulama, a Congo village. This photograph illustrates the depopulation of Congo villages. Mr. Whiteside writes: 'About five years ago, Lulama had between 3,000 and 4,000 inhabitants but by constant oppression and murders on the part of the ABIR. sentries, the population has now decreased to less than 100.' Casement visited Lulama on 31ʰ August 1903.

the rubber growing districts, preferring to live as refugees rather than to live under such brutal treatment. Of course, some of the de-population must also have been caused by the high death-rate involved in the red rubber collection system itself.

On the 6th August Casement took twelve paddlers up Nakaka Creek leaving the *Henry Reed* behind. There he heard reports of flogging. The regular whipping of Africans was also common. They were tied down spread-eagled and whipped with a chicotte for as many as fifty or 100 lashes. African distrust of government officials was seen when people fled from the party until they learned 'we were Mission folk and not from Government, they returned.'[14]

At the end of August and the beginning of September Casement spent time in the towns of Bonginda and Bongandanga, both of which had European presences. The CBM had a large mission station at Bonginda, and so often on trips taken in September, Casement was joined by CBM missionaries, showing again his close relationship with this group. On the 29th August Casement records: 'Arrived Bongandanga. Saw rubber market, nothing by guns – about 20 armed men. The people 242 men with rubber all guarded like convicts. To call this "trade" is the height of lying.'[15] Casement also encountered the system of hostage taking which was regularly used in the region. Often women were taken prisoner to ensure the good behaviour and cooperation of the men in working. Casement was moved by what he saw to write: 'Infamous, infamous, shameful system.'[16]

At the beginning of September one of the contested incidents occurred which would be used by the Belgians to discredit Casement and his report. Henri Spelier was a Belgian agent at Lulanga. He had passed Bonginda by boat during the time of Casement's visit there and he had been the object of what be considered to be insulting shouts from Africans on the shore. According to Spelier the Africans had cried that the regime of violence had come to an end, that only the English would be left, and that all the others ought to die. Spelier attested that two Englishmen heard these shouts without intervening. There were in fact three white men on the beach, Casement, Danielsen, and Steel, who was another CBM missionary and engineer. Danielsen had, according to one witness, tried to stop the shouting. According to Spelier's report, CBM missionaries had sponsored a rumour that the British State would drive away the Belgians to replace them with Englishmen, and that rubber work would be finished in a few months.[17] Casement's diary for 12 December states: 'Congo has begun their anti-Casement campaign. Cuvelier, a Congo official, launched his first dart against me over the Spelier incident.'[18]

'Home life on the Congo as it ought to be.' A Lolanga scene.

Dft

Africa 40.

Congo Consulat
13 Oct. 1903

My Lord with reference to my despatch
the effect.

The Engineer who gave me his services, the Reverend
X J. Danielson (a Dane) a member of the Congo Balolo
Mission who was on his way home invalided when
I got the "Henry Reed" at Bolobo on 20th July also
refused to accept any remuneration whatsoever.

Mr Danielson's services were of the very greatest
value: indeed without his help I could not have
proceeded very far on my journey.

Casement.

Fragment of the letter from Casement to the Foreign Office.

The Belgians would make other attempts to discredit Casement and his report. His connection with various British missionary societies during his investigation was the point at which he was most vulnerable. Although it is debatable in what manner missionaries were involved in the imperialist schemes of their home governments, a too close connection with them would appear damaging to Casement. For this reason all mention of missionary assistance was taken out of the Casement Report. Only in his private diaries can we see how reliant Casement was on missionary help. As one of the editors of Casement's diary of 1903, Séamas Ó Síocháin, has noted: 'It became clear to me when analysing Casement's up-river movements how heavy his reliance was on missionary groups; Danielsen was one part of this reliance.'[19]

Casement's appreciation of Danielsen

In a letter to the British foreign secretary, the marquess of Lansdowne, Casement gave his own evaluation of Danielsen's importance to his enterprise:

My Lord,

The engineer who gave me the service, the Reverend D. J. Danielson (a Dane) [*sic*], a member of the Congo Balolo Mission, who was on his way home invalided when I got the *Henry Reed* at Bolobo on 20th July alas refused to accept any remuneration whatsoever. Mr. Danielson's services were of the very greatest value: indeed without his help I could not have proceeded very far on my journey. The *Henry Reed* is one of the oldest vessels still navigating the Upper Congo having been launched in 1885. I think it was chiefly due to Mr. Danielson's skill and hard work that she was kept running so long with me on board. As it was we sprang a leak coming down river on 13th September and apart from other consideration I do not think it would have been possible to have the vessel continues running much longer. Had it not been for the help thus afforded me by the A.B.M.U. [American Baptist Missionary Union] and by the Congo Balolo Mission my journey to the Upper Congo could scarcely have been carried out, for to have gone on a Congo Government vessel would have been really useless.

I would beg that I might right to be authorised to make a small grant to the funds of both the Missions which gave such kindly help to my journey. I would suggest that £25 might be given to the A.B.M.U and £20 to the Congo Balolo Mission in the former case as a slight recognition of the service rendered by the free loan of *Henry Reed* and in the latter as an acknowledgement of the help and assistance so spontaneously given by Mr. D. J. Danielson. And I should like to convey my thanks to that Mission with a small grant in aid of its funds, if your Lordship sanctions my doing so, while Mr. Danielson is at home.[20]

Danielsen's obvious skill as an engineer is in evidence in Casement's praise of him.

Casement noted in his diary evidence of Danielsen's quick temper:

25 July – 12.45. Moto, the boy of Danielson cut his foot aft at the pump. D goes and "cuffs the lug [i.e. ear]" of one of the boys Nimpokwa only adding to the trouble.

28 July – 9.20 Another row between Danielson & Nimpokwa and the steering boy Ngolo. It won't do.[21]

Alice Harris noted that relations between the engineer and African workers on board the streamers could be contentious although as already noted this ill-temper was not the same as the violent extremes Sawyers accused him of.

Typical mission steamer crew. Most of the crew were on-board to collect the wood needed for fuelling the engine. This picture shows the S.S. Livingstone *and its crew.*

CHAPTER 4
BACK IN BRITAIN

After assisting Casement, Danielsen took the first ship to England and arrived about 12 October 1903. However, Danielsen's health was not good. Towards the end of his journey with Casement he became quite unwell.[1] This may have been a factor in his return as well as a need to clear any lingering misunderstandings about the accusations made against him.

Danielsen's first action once back in Britain was to go before the Executive Council of the CBM and acquaint them with the details of what he and Casement had witnessed on their journey together. Danielsen then went to Scotland for some months. While in Scotland Danielsen did not neglect the Congo issue. He spoke at several public meetings in Edinburgh and Glasgow. He used not only his first-hand knowledge of the situation, but also photographs, which are repeatedly referred to in various letters, illustrating the injures of some of the atrocity victims. Danielsen was keen to put into action the information which he had gathered. Casement also took a number of steps immediately on his return to England, and it is possible that he had discussed some of his future plans with Danielsen, and possibly they had also discussed the various arguments against the administration of the Free State that might be placed before a British public. He certainly gave permission for Danielsen to make use of the information collected while travelling together as soon as the latter came to England.[2]

The CBM Position

Danielsen was eager to force the CBM to start a Congo campaign immediately and appealed to the mission to do so. Danielsen recounted the journey that he and Casement had taken and the likely conclusions on Casement's report. Still the Home Council 'unanimously decided to await the arrival of Mr. Casement – the British Consul to the Congo – before using the information brought home by Mr. Danielson of recent atrocities and the continued maladministration of the Congo State.'[3]

Dr. Grattan Guinness was not unaware of the accusations of atrocities in the Congo. As early as 1896 the Home Council addressed the issue:

An important communication from Mr. Sjöblom was received and presented to the Council, and it was decided that a communication should be made to the

Congo Secretary in Brussels on the subject, making a clear statement as to the facts of Congo atrocities at all of the varied Mission Stations.

There had been criticism of the governance in the Congo, especially from missionaries; but they had had no special effect, because they were isolated incidents. To have an effect it was necessary to have an organised campaign

The Swedish Baptist missionary, E. V. Sjöblom, another alumnus of Harley College, was perhaps Leopold's most forceful critic in the late 1890s, speaking to all who would listen and publishing a detailed attack on the Congo's regime of rubber terror in the Swedish press in 1896, an attack that was picked up by newspapers in other countries. Guinness had been so moved with the horror of the situation that he went to Brussels in 1896 where he met had King Leopold.[4] He presented the ghastly facts of the case to the king. But his argument had been more economic than humanitarian. He later wrote:

Sjöblom with a slaughtered elephant. The photograph was taken by his wife shortly before his death.

I further enlarged on the suicidal policy, pursued by so many of the State agents, of "killing the goose that lays the golden egg," for, as I explained, only the native can work in such a climate. The King seemed greatly interested and pained by what I had to say, and subsequently humanitarian recommendations were sent to the Congo, with the effect that, of recent years, as our missionaries are concerned, the smoked [i.e. cut] hands are entirely a matter of the past.[5]

The king's response had been to set up a commission to appease public opinion:

> Stung by the mounting criticism, Leopold reacted by setting up, in September 1896, the Commission for the protection of the Natives with six members, three Catholic and three Protestant missionaries (including the prominent British Baptists, George Grenfell and William Bentley). With its members stationed far apart, however, and not given any transport or administrative support, the Commission remained a paper entity. Atrocity stories continued.[6]

The CBM council had described their satisfaction with the setting up of the commission:

> The proposed reforms by the Free State Government were discussed and the Council noted with pleasure that Mr. Grenfell, Mr. Bentley and Dr. Sims together with one of the Roman Catholic missionaries have been appointed to investigate any case of oppression of the natives or cruelty on the part of the State officials that may be reported to them, such investigations to be reported to the Government.[7]

Guinness was completely won over to the King's position and became an important advocate for the Congo Free State:

> This desire to appease is most clearly exemplified by Guinness. Because of his eagerness to expand his mission, there were times when he maintained a continuous contact with Brussels and Antwerp. On these occasions he did not neglect to point out how well the authorities and the missions were now working together in the field.[8]

Obviously the meeting with King Leopold had made a striking impact on Grattan Guinness personally. Leopold was known to be a very charming man and often won support by acting the part of the enchanting host for his guests. Guinness felt he had protested in a civilised way and his grievances had been properly addressed. As late as 17 October 1902 Guinness had written to Morel, still maintaining, 'There are certain benefits such as religious freedom under Belgian rule, which cannot be obtained under French administration.'[9] Although this position was an anathema to Morel he was reliant on missionary information:

Morel and Fox Bourne, another reform campaigner, realized that they needed British missionaries to testify against the Congo Free State in order to persuade the British public and, in turn, the government to take up their case. Morel approached the BMS [Baptist Missionary Society] in 1901 and was rebuffed in the light of its effort to win approval from the Congo Free State for further expansion into the Congo interior.[10]

Although the meeting with the king had made an impact, so did the other ambitions of the CBM on Guinness's position. In 1902 Guinness had given Morel the hard-headed assessment that the British government was not likely to intervene, so any public protest by his missionaries would only undermine their long term evangelical goals. Morel describes the tiring work of getting information from the CBM:

The sphere of the work of the Congo Balolo Mission lying almost in the rubber district, I wrote direct to Dr. Harry Grattan Guinness, the Director of that Mission. He replied (November 8, 1902) very courteously, to the effect that his Mission had a good deal of information, but until its attitude was clearly defined, there would be unwisdom in publicity. He added that the matter would be brought forward at the next meeting of the Council. I wrote again at once, A few days later I wrote a further letter. The reply indicated the existence of doubts in the writer's mind as to whether any practical good could ensue from the systematic exposure. In answer to an enquiry the ensuing month, I was informed that the Council had been too much occupied with business of an important character to concern itself with the matter under discussion, and that the amount of information at its disposal was not, in point of fact, considerable. Dr. Guinness (December 1902) went on to say that he had complained personally to King Leopold in 1896 about the treatment of the natives and that the mass of proof he had placed before the latter resulted in humanitarian instructions being sent out to officials. I gathered from this correspondence that the Council of the Congo Balolo Mission found themselves in some difficulty. But I had no doubt that they would ultimately be brought to see that they must speak out or allow their missionaries on the spot to do so. And this was what happened before very many months had passed.[11]

On 5 February 1903 the Congo Administration had appeared on the agenda at the meeting of the Congo Council of the CBM. Morel had requested that the Council would place at his disposal the information in their hands with reference to the treatment of natives by the State. It had been decided that Guinness should conduct interviews with the relevant persons (one of them was probably Henry Fox Bourne, the leader of the Aborigines Protection Society), 'after which the Council will decide whether it will be advisable to place our information in Mr. Morel's hands.'[12] The next meeting of the Council had taken place on 26 February 1903. It had not been possible for Guinness to meet the persons mentioned, and dealing with Morel's request had been postponed. At the next meeting on the 26 March 1903 the request had not been mentioned at all. Instead it had been noted in the minute book:

The matter of Congo Atrocities was again considered and it was felt that the time had arrived for us to make some statement relative to them. Dr. Guinness was therefore, asked to kindly undertake to write an article for publication in the Regions Beyond stating clearly our present position and future policy regarding the above.[13]

It is probable that this step had been an excuse for not giving Morel the material he had asked for. The article was published in *Regions Beyond* in April 1903.[14] It is quite moderate. It admits the atrocities, but places the main responsibility for them on the local sentries and not on the authorities and absolutely not on King Leopold. Up to this point it appears that Guinness had been treading carefully in order to avoid causing offence.[15] The article was named: 'The indictment against the Congo Administration. Is it True?' It falls back on racist stereotypes, arguing that:

the native… does not care for hard work of any description, having been trained for countless generations to an easy-going life suited to the climate and to the prolific generosity of surrounding Nature… This antipathy of the native for work, be it freely acknowledged, is an unfortunate trait of his character, and both education and Christianity must gradually modify this condition before we can expect to find a strenuous type of manhood developed.[16]

It is a classic example of missionary argument from the period: only when Christianity and civilisation are accepted can the African hope to make real progress. Guinness goes on to argue that the methods used by the authorities to extract rubber are unacceptable, and the payment given is an 'absolute absurd figure'.

Morel thought that the missionaries were too timid in their relations with the Congo government and too bold in trying to exploit the reform movement for sectarian purposes. 'I feel extremely tired by these fearful missionaries', he wrote in 1903. '…[their] attitude is disgraceful.'[17] His antipathy focused particularly on Grattan Guinness '[his] conduct has not been, in my opinion straightforward,' Morel wrote to Holt in January 1904. '…He has kept silent for 10 years. Not only does he keep silent like the other Executives of the Mission; but he prevented, or at any rate threw cold water on Fox Bourne's persistent and courageous crusade.'[18] Within a year however, the Congo Balolo Mission would give up hope that the Congo Free State would permit expansion, and Guinness would ally himself with Morel, despite their ideological differences.[19]

A guard of the forest with two prisoners. The first atrocity photograph in Regions Beyond *in April 1903.*

Danielsen's campaign

After meeting with the CBM Home Council, Danielsen left London to spend some time in Scotland. He had contacts in Glasgow from his time there, and naturally he was invited to speak at Christian meetings on his experiences in the Congo. Given that the Congo Free State had become a matter of national interest, Danielsen's experiences would have been of interest to his audience. Roger Casement had given him permission to speak freely about what he had witnessed with him. His words would have had a powerful impact. Danielsen was a very charismatic speaker. Later in the Faroes at his evangelistic services both he and his audience would be overcome with sobbing. In addition, the material that the missionaries had was extremely emotive.

Missionaries who returned routinely addressed public meetings. At the turn of the century, attending such meetings was much more widespread. Without radio, television or film, they might provide entertainment; however, they were also educational. Dr. Harry Grattan Guinness also began a lecture tour of the country some time after he had changed his position on the Congo Free State and the cause had become so celebrated. Both he and his father were renowned as preachers, and they could guarantee large audiences. These speaking tours would not only engage people with the issues, they would also prove excellent fund-raising opportunities for the CBM.[20]

Some of the most prolific speakers would be John and Alice Harris, CBM missionaries in the Congo. Particularly effective in their meetings would be the magic lantern shows, with pictures to show the types of atrocities the alleged by the missionaries. In a pre-television age, and with cinema in its infancy, such visual images had a profound effect on audiences in Europe and America.[21] The extremity of those from the Congo would create a reaction. It was partly what would lead the Congo Reform Association (CRA), which Morel, Grattan Guinness, and Casement would found in 1904, to be eventually successful.

Too much attention?

Morel quickly learned of Danielsen's return and was eager to publish any information he may have had. He wrote to Guinness on 13 October 1903, only a couple of days after Danielsen's return to England. The answer from Guinness is dated 16 October 1903 and contains the first information about the atrocity photos used in this campaign:

One of our engineers, Mr. Danielson, has just returned from the Congo. During two months before he left West Africa he accompanied His Majesty's British

Consul, Mr. Casement, on a special tour of inspection through the territory of the ABIR. Co.

Mr. Casement is now on his way home to England, returning not by the lower Congo but passing from Brazzaville through French territories and thence to the coast. I have no doubts that he has made a series of communications to the government, and that on his return Lord Lansdowne and he will be in a conference. Naturally Mr. Danielson saw exactly the same things as the Consul observed, and made his own notes.

I understand from him that the Consul enjoined of him caution in speaking of what he had seen whilst still in Africa, but told him that once in the old country he was free to make use of any information he had gleaned. The question is whether or not we shall publish this matter in the next issue for "Regions Beyond" or in what way the Council of our Mission will suggest that we may best employ the information.

If we decide to write a special article in Regions Beyond, the journal of the mission, I have illustrations of dreadful character which I can use, showing cruelty, not only in the past, but actually inside the last few months I possess three terrible pictures of mutilations. In the event of your wishing to republish anything we put into "Regions Beyond" we shall be glad to let you have blocks.

I am sure that the only hesitancy that my friends might feel would be to entrench in any way upon the information to be conveyed by the British Consul to the Government, but from what Mr. Danielson affirms concerning the latter we have that gentleman's permission to make use of the facts that have come to their notice, it may be that we shall see our way to print immediately. I will let you know this day week what our decision in this matter.[22]

Guinness's uncertain stance can still be found in this letter. Although the information had been conveyed to the Home Council they had not taken any definite steps with regards to a new policy towards the Congo Free State.

Danielsen and Morel commenced a direct correspondence from November onwards. Morel writes:

My dear Sir,

I have your letter of the 14th, enclosing postal order value 3/6d. I have sent you, under separate cover, a copy of the issue of the *West African Mail* containing Mr. Week's letters, and also a copy of the last issue. I will send you the 5 successive issues, according to your request. I am also sending you a dozen copies of *The Congo Slave State* to your Glasgow address as desired.

Of course I have had conversation and correspondence with Dr. Grattan Guinness about your information. My feeling is that Government or no Government we should lose no further time in publishing the information,

I think the delay weakens our case. I have told Dr. Grattan Guinness so, but each man must judge for himself. The idea now is to postpone the publication of your matter until January, when it is to appear simultaneously in the *Regions Beyond* journal, and the *West African Mail*, but I have asked Dr. Grattan Guinness if he can place some of your photographs at my disposal before that date, perhaps you will write him to the same effect?

At any rate you can send him a copy of this letter if you like. I hope each photograph has a history to it, otherwise it will give the enemy a chance to try and discredit them.

You mention that on the 7th and 8th inst, you were speaking before 4 or 5,000 people in Edinburgh. I wish it were possible (I speak with all respect) to infuse into your missionaries some notion of how to get at the ear of the public in connection with a matter of this kind. Now who knows what you said to those 4 or 5,000 people? Not a soul outside your immediate audience. But if you had had press representatives there, your words would have been reproduced all over the country. The thing is to get these statements into the paper, and to rouse public opinion. If they are not got into the papers, public opinion will never be roused, and the whole agitation, I assert deliberately, depends for its success upon maintaining unimpaired and connected interest on the part of public opinion; that can only be done through the press, and I don't think you gentlemen realise the fact sufficiently. Now if you like to give me a short summary of what you said in connection with Congo maladministration before those 4 or 5,000 people, I will publish it in my paper; and do, the next time you are speaking, arrange to have representatives of the press present. What I am writing you now I have said verbally to Dr. Grattan Guinness. This battle must be fought with a continuous systematic attack; not by a short attack and then a retreat to consider the next step, but blow after blow that is the only way to keep up sustained public interest. Needless to say I shall be grateful and pleased for any information you may give me at any time on this subject, whether you write from Africa or from Europe.[23]

The initial outcome of this promise of cooperation would be the first of a series of press articles in which Danielsen lamented the atrocities in the Congo. It would give him public attention – not all of it desirable.

CHAPTER 5
PRESS ATTENTION

The account of Danielsen's Edinburgh speeches that Morel had suggested he write appeared in the latter's journal, *West African Mail*:

CONGO STATE
WILL EUROPE AWAKE TOO LATE?
Mr. D. J. Danielson on the Congo Horror.
"EVERY MAN, WOMAN AND CHILD IN THE RUBBER DISTRICTS – A SLAVE!"
WILL THEY KILL US BEFORE THEY GO AWAY?
Special to the West African Mail
(From a Correspondent)

Mr. D. J. Danielson, who is attached to the Regions Beyond Missionary Society, on the Congo, has in the course of the last few weeks addressed several meetings in Edinburgh on the subject of Congo State misrule. On one occasion three thousand people assembled at the Synod Hall to hear Mr. Danielson speak.

Women held hostage in chains to encourage their husbands to bring in larger quantities of rubber.

In the course of his speech at the Synod Hall, Mr. Danielson denounced in the strongest language the abominable oppression to which the Congo natives are subjected. The rubber trade – if it should be called trade – declared Mr. Danielson, was rapidly killing off the natives, and would end in the virtual extermination of all the Congo races, whom the Congo State was able to get in the grip. A Free State by name, it was a Slave state in fact. Mr. Danielson explained that he had just come home from the Congo. He had been living for upwards of two years in the Upper Congo, in one of the rubber districts where the Belgian Concessionaires were carrying on their atrocious rubber traffic with the help of the State officers, for concessionaires and State worked hand in hand. Mr. Danielson went on to say that he had personally witnessed the commitment of abominable deeds, and had on several occasions prevented the Belgians and their soldiers from perpetrating outrages upon men and women. He had photos in his possession illustrating these atrocities upon the natives, atrocities perpetrated this very year, and arising from the rubber extortion. It had been said, that the

CUTTING OFF OF NATIVES' HANDS

was done by Congo State soldiers to account for the number of cartridges they expended – one hand for each cartridge. But he thought the chief purpose of these mutilations was to strike terror into the natives to show them what they had to

Rubber collectors with their baskets.

expect if they failed to satisfy the white man's demands for rubber, rations and other taxes. "It is a daily sight," said Mr. Danielson "to see

Women Tied Up As Hostages

and kept sometimes for many weeks – tied up with strong rope so that they shall not manage to steal away to their homes."

Mr. Danielson further asserted that every man, woman and child in the rubber districts of Congo State was "kept a slave, and a slave of the lowest order," and that the natives were far better off before King Leopold had anything to do with the country. "The cry of the natives," continued Mr. Danielson, was "When will the white rubber collectors be satisfied? When will they have enough rubber? When will they leave our country, and leave us in peace?"

"Will They Kill Us All Before They Go Away?"

These were questions said Mr. Danielson, frequently asked, and how could they be answered?

"Several natives," declared Mr. Danielson, "asked me before I left for home, if I could tell their bad circumstances to the good white men in the far-off country, and ask them to help and to deliver them from their taskmasters." "With God's help," continued the speaker, "I will tell everyone I can of this terrible slavery which is carried out in the Congo State. If this atrocious Administration goes on much longer, in a few years' time whole districts will have become entirely and absolutely depopulated. Then Europe will awake. But it will be too late."

"Moral And Material Regeneration"

Mr. Danielson reiterated that the curse of the whole business was the rubber taxes. The natives often told him that in the old days they used to have some happy days, even when actual cannibalism reigned unchecked, but that since the rubber collectors have come in to the country, they had not one happy day. They were living in misery, slavery and poverty, a prey to sickness and disease – a poor, miserable people that once used to be so prosperous.

England's Duty

"We preach to the people the Love of God. They ask us, Why does He then allow these men to ill-treat us like this? Why does He not deliver us from these tyrants? I say, how can we answer these reasonable questions? May this country, which God has made so great, help these outraged natives; The Congo races are fine races, but they are being decimated and destroyed."[1]

Reuters

In fact very quickly interest began to grow in Danielsen. The Congo issue had been kept in the press for some time by Morel's clever campaign. Journalists knew the British consul had conducted a survey and were eager for any information they could publish. On 7 December 1903, six days after Casement had landed in England, the *Daily Mirror* published this article about his survey:

Danielsen held his first meeting concerning the Congo in Edinburgh's Synod Hall.

Horrors of the Congo
British Official Finds Terrible Slavery in the Belgian State

The terrible condition of the natives in the Belgian Congo State attained the dimensions of a scandal some time ago and the British Government appointed Mr. R. Casement, the British Consul, to undertake a tour of personal observation.

Mr. Casement has now completed his mission, says Reuter, after travelling over a thousand miles into the rubber districts, and he is now engaged in drawing up his report for the Foreign Office, which will shortly be in the hands of the Government.

The consular tour was to have lasted six months, but after the expiration of two months the scenes witnessed and the information obtained were of such a character that it was decided that further evidence was unnecessary. Ample confirmation of terrible abuses has been obtained.

It will be shown on the undeniable authority of a British official that the most horrible outrages is still being perpetrated under the rubber regime and that Slavery and barbarism in the most revolting form forms exist today. For the present the lips of those who have witnessed these things are sealed, but an Englishman who was with the British Consul during the whole of his tour sums up the situation as follows: 'The most terrible slavery exists. The administration is atrocious, and if there is no speedy intervention it will be too late.'[2]

TO-DAY'S WEATHER.

Our special forecast for to-day is: Cold and fair at first; southerly winds, with rain later.

Lighting-up time for all vehicles, 4.25.

SEA PASSAGES.

English Channel, smooth to moderate; North Sea, smooth; Irish Channel, rather rough.

The Daily Mirror.

34ist Day of Year. Monday, Dec. 7, 1903. 24 days to Dec. 31.

PAGE 3.

1903-04.	December.				January.	
Sun.	...	13	20	27	...	3
Mon.	7	14	21	28	...	4
Tues.	8	15	22	29	...	5
Wed.	9	16	23	30	...	6
Thurs.	10	17	24	31	...	7
Fri.	11	18	25	...	1	8
Sat.	12	19	26	...	2	9

To-Day's News at a Glance.

Home.

A fog of great density covered London and other parts of the country on Saturday, impeding traffic and stopping sport.—See page 5.

The Swansea Corporation Tramways Committee have accepted the British tender for the local tramways extension, involving an outlay of £103,000. The German tender was £2,000 less in the aggregate amount.

Five hundred young salmon have been put into the Thames at Teddington.

Lady Constance Mackenzie has arrived in Texas on her way to a friend's ranch, where she intends to hunt wild pigs. A correspondent says Lady Constance recently engaged in a wolf hunt.

Mr. A. F. Jeffreys, M.P., who met with an accident while hunting about a month ago, has had a relapse and is still confined to his bed.

Dr. Neocles Kasasis, rector of Athens University, is now on a visit to Oxford.

The British M.P.'s and their wives are having a pleasant time in the Riviera. Speaking at a dinner at Nice M. Arago, a deputy, said, "May we, to quote a celebrated 'mot,' say one day, 'There is no longer any Channel.'"

Mr. C. N. Wilkinson, the Secretary of the North Eastern Railway Co., has resigned owing to failing health.

Captain Thomas C. Dutton, of the Cunard Liner Umbria, sailed from Liverpool on Saturday for his last voyage as a shipmaster. On his return from America three weeks hence he will retire on a pension, after fifty years' service.

The London County Council hopes to open the New Cross electric tramway line by the end of this year.

Two Progressive candidates have been returned at the Marylebone Borough Council bye-elections.

At their annual dinner the Newbury Volunteer Fire Brigade subscribed nearly £5 in aid of the employees of the local theatre, which was burnt down last week.

The cremation of the body of Sir John Richard Robinson, formerly editor and manager of the "Daily News," took place on Saturday at Golder's Green, and the ashes were subsequently interred at Highgate Cemetery.

The Western divisions of the Channel and Home Fleets, under Rear-Admirals Lambton and Poe, arrived at Plymouth yesterday to grant Christmas leave to their crews.

The unknown man found on the Brighton sea esplanade recently, and who died at the Sussex County Hospital, has been identified as Mr. William Mathie, of Glasgow.

Mr. George Wyndham, Chief Secretary for Ireland, states that there is no foundation for the rumour that he is not likely to seek re-election for Dover.

The London Stock Exchange was closed on Saturday.

Obituary.

Alderman Brigden died at Brighton yesterday in his ninetieth year.

Mr. A. W. Wills, brother of Mr. Justice Wills, has died at his residence at Wylde-green, near Birmingham.

Mr. T. Eustace Smith, who was from 1868 until 1885 Liberal member of Parliament for Tynemouth, has died abroad.

Mrs. Martha Jeffries has died at Wick, near Bristol, at the age of 101. She had been sextoness of Wick Church since the consecration on April 3, 1850.

The death has occurred of the Rev. Richard H. Killick, who, when King Edward brought a Danish Princess to London for his bride, received her at Temple Bar as Rector of St. Clement Dane's, Strand, the former site of a colony of her countrymen.

Colonial.

Telegrams from Peking state that in official circles there is great excitement over the British expedition to Tibet.

A public meeting held at Salisbury, Rhodesia, on Thursday decided to ask the ...

Social.

Prince Alexander of Teck, who is engaged to Princess Alice of Battenberg, does not go to South Africa with the reserve squadron of the 7th Hussars, but joins the depôt at Canterbury.

Princess Christian arrived at Hatfield yesterday on a visit to Lord Mountstephen at Brocket Hall.

Princess Louise Augusta of Schleswig-Holstein sailed from Plymouth on Saturday on the Orient Pacific Liner Ormuz for Colombo.

Foreign.

The Tsaritsa, completely recovered, and the Tsar are again in St. Petersburg.

Ex-Queen Natalie of Servia has arrived at Belgrade to visit the grave of her murdered son Alexander.

Wrapped in the flags of the two countries, the signed treaty for the Panama Canal has been returned by Panama to the United States. The chest containing the document was carried from the Palace to the United States Consulate in Panama by policemen.

M. Pleske, Russian Minister of Finance, is so seriously ill that Professor von Miculiez has been summoned from Breslau for consultation.

Yvette Guilbert, who has been lying ill for several months at Steglitz, near Berlin, has been able to undertake her return journey to Paris, but she will not perform for a time.

Owing to vast increase in the traffic of the Berlin City Electric Railway, trains will now run with intervals of only 2½ minutes, weekdays and Sundays. London has not quite reached this stage of public convenience.

At the municipal savings bank of Cagli, in Italy, a deficit of £12,000 has been discovered. All the clerks at the bank have been placed under arrest.

The Etruria is taking to England a silver table service for the Erin, subscribed for in the United States as a national testimonial to Sir Thomas Lipton.

A gang of forgers has been captured in Boston, United States, the leader being a man named Schmidt, who said he had escaped conviction for Bank of England forgeries by becoming an informer.

The island of Heligoland has been put in telephonic connection with Berlin.

A duel between M. Thomoguex and M. Barré, two skilled swordsmen, took place near Paris on Saturday.—See page 5.

The American cotton market, after three days' panic, has become quiet. There was no repetition of the scenes of excitement on Saturday, and prices changed only slightly. The Chinese cotton crop this season is a splendid one.

Archbishop Bourne has postponed his departure from Rome for London until Saturday morning, and he will not arrive here until the 19th or 20th.

Law and Police Courts.

Sentence of penal servitude for life was passed at Leeds Assizes upon Edward North, aged twenty-nine, a labourer, who was found guilty of having attempted to murder Dr. George White, junior medical officer at Sheffield Union Workhouse, by striking out at him with a knife whilst undergoing examination at his hands.

A breach of promise action brought at the Glamorganshire Assizes by Lilian Maud Gough, hotel manageress, against George Whittington has been settled by the defendant consenting to a judgment for £250.

Giuseppi Frattanoli, an Italian, was sentenced to twenty-one days' hard labour at the North London Police Court on Saturday for sending a boy out to beg with an accordion and a monkey.

Court Circular.

Sandringham, Sunday, Dec. 6.

THE BROKEN TRAIN.

Wild Dash Down Shap Fell.

AN EXPRESS WRECKED

Providential Escape of the Passengers.

A railway accident, extraordinary in some respects, that might have had disastrous consequences but for the forethought of a signalman, occurred on Saturday ... Carlisle, on the London and ... Railway.

The couplings of a fast go... North from Liverpool to Carl... the race down the steep grad... summit to Penrith, and the ... wagons ran on, leaving thir... a van behind. These overto... with the forepart of the train ... the result that four wagons w...

The 1 a.m. Scottish ex... North—which runs from Ca... without stopping—dashed int... the engine severing itself fron... all seven coaches being thro...

Of the seventeen passenge... one was hurt; but the driver ... George Bates, of Crewe, was ... about the head and arms. ... veyed the passengers to their ...

The express from Scotl... Euston six hours late; and ... don to the North on Saturday ... delayed.

The Race Down Shap Fell.

The incidents which followe... two parts of the fast goods ... citing they should be narr... detail, as they presented th... only spectator, viz., the signa... at Egmont Junction.

The engine as it went by, ... only a van and two wagons at... in a few seconds the thirty ot... the van came thundering pas... and uncontrolled force down ... stantly the signalman sent w... next box, at Keswick Junct... branch to Keswick and W... leaves the main line.

The man in that box sho... signal to the driver, telling hi... was divided. The driver's ... that signal was to continue ... keep in front of the pursuing ... a hundred yards outside ... the chasing vans caught up ... vehicles.

Then came the terrible cras... the impetus of the enginele... the noise was heard a mile dis...

It occurred almost beneat... pedestrian and vehicular tra... instant the wreckage piled ... and the merchandise, which i... of frozen mutton, was strewn ... manent way.

It was on towards this perilo... flying Scotch express came r... speed.

How the Express was Saved.

The moment the severed train had passed his box the Keswick Junction signalman turned to "danger" the signal governing the north entrance to the station.

George Bates, of Crewe, the driver, saw the signal-arm go up just as he was close to it. He shut off steam to slow down, but the train ran round the sharp curve which shuts off the view of the station from the north, and went with great force into the wagons which were fouling the up line.

Flames rushed from the firebox and severely burned Bates, who was thrown off the footplate on to the side of the metals, but not before he had secured the situation.

The engine continued to run about a hundred yards ...

saloon; the whole, in railway language, being equal to eight and a half vehicles. Everyone of these, except the last pair of wheels of the rear van, left the metals, but none of them fell over.

The Passengers Show Gratitude.

Among the seventeen passengers by the Scotch express were Viscount Brackley, son of the Earl of Ellesmere, Mr. Falconer, Chairman of the Mersey Railway, and also (he deserves particular mention) a soldier, who slept unaroused through the fearful crash.

An impromptu meeting was held on the platform, and as a token of their gratitude Lord Brackley and Mr. Falconer gave £5 each to the station-master for the benefit of the injured driver, who was suffering acutely from his burned head, hands, and legs. ...

HORRORS OF THE CONG

British Official Finds Terri... Slavery in the Belgian State

The terrible condition of the natives in ... Belgian Congo State attained the dim... sions of a scandal some time ago, and ... British Government appointed Mr. R. C... ment, the British Consul, to undertak... tour of personal observation.

Mr. Casement has now completed his ... sion, says Reuter, after travelling ove... thousand miles into the rubber districts, ... he is now engaged in drawing up his re... for the Foreign Office, which will shortly ... in the hands of the Government.

The Consular tour was to have lasted ... months, but at the expiration of two mo... the scenes witnessed and the information ... tained were of such a character that it ... decided that further evidence was unne... sary. Ample confirmation of terrible ab... has been obtained.

It will be shown on the undeniable au... rity of a British official that the most horr... outrages are still being perpetrated u... the rubber regimé, and that slavery and ... barism in the most revolting forms exist ... day.

For the present the lips of those who h... witnessed these things are sealed, but ... Englishman, who was with the Bri... Consul during the whole of his tour, s... up the situation as follows:—

"The most terrible slavery exists. ... administration is atrocious, and if ther... not speedy intervention it will be too la...

... The race with the mails between the Cunard steamer Lucania and the American liner St. Paul ended greatly in favour of the Cunard boat. The Lucania's letters reached London in time for delivery at 9.30 a.m. on Saturday, so enabling the replies to be despatched by the Cunard steamer Umbria, which left Liverpool in the afternoon. The St. Paul did not arrive at Southampton till long after the Umbria had started with the replies.

LORD MAYOR AND PAUPER ALIENS.

Another example of the pauper alien invasion attracted notice at the Mansion House Police Court on Saturday. Two Germans, neither of whom could speak English, were charged with being on premises in Aldgate with felonious intentions.

"It's a marvel to me," said the Lord Mayor, ...

The front page of the Daily Mirror *of the 7th of December carried an article with the headline "Horrors of the Congo". This appeared six days after Roger Casement's arrival from Congo.*

The 'Englishman' referred is evidently Danielsen, as he had been the only European with Casement for his whole tour. The quotation appears to be a loose summary of the final sentences of the fourth section in his *West African Mail* article of the previous week.[3] Reuters had evidently assumed that Danielsen was English, either when they had telegrammed him, or when they had 'improved' the sentences from the *West African Mail*. The latter hypothesis seems the more likely, for Danielsen, it would appear, was not pleased by the Reuters' report. In a letter that is now lost, he wrote to Morel about it, and in his reply Morel had called the Reuters' paragraph 'absurd' – obviously agreeing Danielsen's sim-

Carrubers Close Mission building in Edinburgh where Danielsen also held a meeting.

ilar assessment.[4] Reuters had attempted to interview Casement on Saturday 5 December, but had gone ahead and released their statement, for two days later Casement had lamented in his diary the appearance of their report in at least one other London newspaper: 'Papers full of my Congo journey. D. M. [*Daily Mirror*] got a leader & Pall Mall [*Pall Mall Gazette*] tonight. Awful mistake.'[5] The newspapers had created complications for him that he had been trying to contain. A few days before Casement had made his entry, Danielsen had written to Morel:

> I have just received a letter from Mr. Casement. He thinks it is best That my name should not be mentioned in connection with his Tour in July Aug & September yet until The Government has Taken steps so if you publish anything of The Cuttings please keep out That piece about the Tour. The Consul tells me that he is glad to see The Congo article in your paper of last week.
>
> I think that we have got The great Congo Beast by The Horns This Time. I will be speaking at Edinburgh at The Carrubers [*sic*] Close Mission on The 19th

and in Synod Hall on the 20th This Month. Good we have also Slides of the Boys with Hands off. They will be shown Then.

I expected to hear news from Congo last Mail, but none. (Men seem to be afraid of the Consequence, if they speak the Truth). I Think That we Missionaries can do very little in Congo State, before this Slavery is brought to a stop.

Yours Sincerely
D. J. Danielson[29]

Casement had only asked Danielsen to keep his name from the papers. He had not asked him to stop the public meetings in Scotland. Morel also agreed to be discreet in his use of Casement's name:

I will do exactly as you wish. I will not mention your name any further. In fact I have cut out from a paragraph which is going in this week a reference to you which has been made by Danielson in a Glasgow newspaper, in which he says that he has been touring the interior with you. I am publishing an extract from Danielson's statement, and I am leaving that part out.

P.S. I suppose you know that Danielson is eager to publish this stuff now that Grattan Guinness is keeping it back until January.[6]

Glasgow newspaper

As Morel's letter indicates, however, it had already been too late to keep Casement's role – if not his name – separate from Danielsen. They had already been linked in an article that had appeared in the Glasgow newspaper, the *Daily Record and Mail*.[7] Danielsen, after his Edinburgh lectures, had been in Glasgow for the annual missionary conference of the Grove Street Institute, at which missionaries from number of countries had spoken over the Saturday and Sunday of the weekend of 28–29 November 1903.[8]

The RBMU had an office in the Institute, which had strong links with Carrubbers Close mission, where he had spoken in Edinburgh, and it was in the mission hall circle in Glasgow.[9] Danielsen in all probability would already be familiar with it from his earlier stay in the city. When he came to Glasgow he had taken the advice of the politically astute Morel to publicise his concerns by speaking to the press. An interview with him had appeared in the *Daily Record and Mail* on the Monday after the conference:

RUBBER SACRIFICES
HORROR OF SLAVERY IN CONGO FREE STATE

Some of the harrowing episodes of slavery so graphically depicted by Harriet Beecher Stowe in "Uncle Tom's Cabin" are vividly recalled by a thrilling story told to a "Record and Mail" representative by Mr. D. J. Danielson, who has just returned from the Congo Free State, where he has been engaged in missionary work, and is in Glasgow for the purpose of enlisting the sympathies of all liberty-loving men and women in the struggle to emancipate the Congo natives from the thraldom of their taskmasters.

"It is called a free state, but it is only nominally free" said Mr. Danielson in describing the country. "The natives are virtually all slaves, as they were compelled to bring in the produce of their labour, such as rubber and ivory, to the Belgian monopolist companies.

"The whole of the Congo is given out to these companies, who have absolute right over the natives and do with them as they please. They mutilate them most horribly if they do not satisfy their demand for rubber. In the State there is supposed to be no forced labour and yet there are 17,000 soldiers or sentries, or 'guards of the forest' as they are called by the authorities, who do nothing but help the rubber companies to compel the natives to bring in rubber.

"One need not wonder," said Mr. Danielson with emphasis, "at the rising of the natives against the State. It is this rubber question that is the cause of all the trouble there. I have in my possession photos of mutilated natives whose hands were cut off as a warning to others who refused to work to the satisfaction of the rubber agents. The parents of a mutilated native remonstrated with one of the rubber companies, and they were told 'if the natives did not work better, the same would be done again.'

"The taking of women as hostages is a daily occurrence, and they are only set at liberty again when their husbands and friends bring in the quantity of rubber demanded by the agents of the companies. The present method of trading is said to be far worse than that of the enslavement of the Arabs which it has displaced. And yet King Leopold who declared fifteen years ago, when he was entrusted with the rulership of the Congo Free State by the European Powers, that 'our only programme is the work of moral and material regeneration.'

"This," added the missionary "is how he has kept his trust."

"In July, August and September of this year," continued Mr. Danielson, "I toured through the Congo with the British Consul stationed there, and his Majesty's representative saw some fearful sights. I am glad to state that the Government is going to take steps within the next few weeks to do something in the matter, and more of the terrible conditions of things in the Congo Free State will then be made known."

In reply to questions by our representative, Mr. Danielson emphatically declared that "if this slavery is not put a stop to the time will come when the natives of the Congo Free State will be entirely exterminated."

"In some places," he further remarked, "the door is shut on missionaries, and one of the conditions on which King Leopold became sovereign of the State was that missionaries of all religions should have full liberty of to preach and travel throughout the country. In several instances steps have been taken to prevent the natives from selling food-stuffs to the missionaries without first obtaining the permission of the rubber monopolists."

Asked why King Leopold did not put a stop to such a statet [*sic*] of things, Mr. Danielson replied that probably the reason was his Majesty "is getting 50 per cent. of all the incomes of the various rubber companies trading in that part of the world. Soldiers and sentries, armed with guns, are placed in rubber villages, as I have indicated, to compel the natives to bring the fruit of their toil to the companies' agents, who pay them what they like for it. The natives live as fugitives and too often become a prey to that dread malady of sleeping sickness."[10]

The following day another part of what was evidently the same interview appeared that took up where the previous one had left off. It dealt with the disease of African trypanosomiasis, or 'sleeping sickness', whose cause (the bite of the tsetse fly) had only been identified earlier in the same year Danielsen was speaking, and therefore probably was not then known to him:

SLEEPING SICKNESS
THE SCOURGE OF THE CONGO FREE STATE

Sleeping sickness is the scourge of the Congo Free State. The mention of it strikes terror into the hearts of the natives, who fly from it as they would before an approaching tornado. Some of its terrible effects were described yesterday to a "Daily Record and Mail" representative by Mr. D. J Danielson, of the Congo Balolo Mission.

Grove Street Institute.

"A great deal of this sleeping sickness, "began Mr. Danielson, is due to insufficiency of food on the part of its victims, who are too often living in a low state and always in dread. The malady is very general, although it is more prevalent on the river banks about 200 miles from the coast."

Describing the first symptoms Mr. Danielson said the victim becomes sleepy and shows a disposition, even when speaking to any of

Dying of sleeping sickness.

his friends, to topple over as in sleep. He keeps himself awake as best he can, while his head rolls from side to side. He also becomes exceedingly immoral, taking to stealing, lying and worse excesses.

"For months," proceeded the speaker, "a sufferer remains in this condition sleeping or half-sleeping all the time, and taking his food fairly well. After that he passes into the second stage, when he has horrible dreams and sees terrible visions. Many of the natives dread this second stage so much that they put cayenne pepper into their eyes to prevent them falling asleep."

"Another stage, and the last one," explained the missionary, "is reached when the victim becomes useless and loses his appetite. The flesh gradually withers of his bones, and he is ultimately a living skeleton. Then, of course, the end is near. A sufferer lingers for twelve, and sometimes eighteen months, during which his pains are of the most intense description."

It was the opinion of Mr. Danielson that if the friends of the poor natives, stricken down with this malady, had time to attend them the deaths would be less numerous than they are. "But the people have to occupy every moment to produce sufficient money to pay the exorbitant taxes the authorities exact from them. The result is the sick victims are entirely neglected."

The opinion was further expressed that if the natives were better fed and better housed the disease would lose much of its virulence when it attacked them.[11]

If Danielsen's syntax as reported in the newspaper is compared with the quotation above from his letter, it can be seen that the journalist had evidently tidied up his remarks. Nevertheless, the combined articles make clear Danielsen's passion, for the first article twice mentions the heat with which he spoke. Implicit in much of he says, as it was in the campaign of the CRA and the involvement of the British government, was the way in which the Congo Free State fell short of the ideals of the European imperial crusade, to civilize and improve the colonized nations. Of course, that it was the foreign regime of the King of Belgium which was degrading the natives and worsening the already terrible effects of sleeping sickness, thereby letting the imperialist side down, made it easier for a British audience to call for reform. More explicit in Danielsen's interview is the political appeal to 'liberty-loving' Britons, who prided themselves on their support of freedom. The interview shows what a coherent and persuasive case Danielsen had developed against the atrocities for a contemporary audience that shared the nonconformist conscience – especially in places like Glasgow – created by the dominant cultural force of evangelicalism. Danielsen's

How the ABIR system destroys the rubber forests

The reproduction from a photograph shows one result of the forced labour system on the Congo. Instead of tapping the vine to obtain rubber this native has cut it down and chopped it into pieces, in his desperate haste to obtain a large supply. The penalty for this act is death – but he is in danger of death anyway. Note the leaves on the ground to catch the juice and the look of hopelessness in the boy's eyes. The vines are now [1905] practically finished round the Abir stations in consequense of this reckless and wasteful method.

appeal was based partly on humanitarian grounds. It highlights the conditions of virtual slavery the people were kept in. For a British public, proud of its campaigns for the abolition of slavery in the previous century, and with its conscience stirred up by the reports of David Livingstone, this was an emotive issue. Danielsen also makes an economic case, stressing the monopolist nature of the rubber companies' trade, which was persuasive to a British public convinced by the contemporary economic doctrine of the necessity of free trade. The punishment of cutting-off of hands is seen as a result of the absolute ownership the traders were able to have over the Congolese. Finally, Danielsen appeals to the wide popular support for the Protestant missionary crusade, for makes it clear that Leopold, contrary to his promises, is blocking missionary access (which Danielsen's audience would understand as *Protestant* ones) to some areas of the Congo. The argument weaves together the contemporary popular founding principles of the Congo Free State as it had been recognised by the Berlin Conference – freedom of religion, free trade, and the abolition of slavery.

Danielsen's Congo campaigning would also feature in the Faroese newspaper, *Tingakrossur*, early in March 1904 when he visited the islands,[12] and these articles will be discussed in chapter 9. It was the first of the Glasgow articles from which Morel published extracts from in his *West African Mail*, on the 11th December, almost a fortnight after the original item had appeared, by which time it had been also reproduced in the *Falkirk Herald* in the same week it had appeared in Glasgow.[13] However much as he supported Danielsen's activity in general, his omissions show which parts of Danielsen's case he possibly felt were politically sensitive. Not only did Morel remove the parts that referred to Casement's activities, he also removed the charge of profiteering that Danielsen had laid against King Leopold in the final paragraph: the king was not merely ignorant of the atrocities committed in his name, but he was mercenary in exploiting human misery. This was no way to speak of a monarch. It was a political radicalism with which many would be uncomfortable. Although Morel would probably not have been troubled by Danielsen's opinion (he was later a Labour MP), he would have realised it was not politic to offend many more conservative individuals by being so outspoken. As will be seen, it was outspokenness such as this, and possibly his more overtly political pronouncements, which would make Danielsen unacceptable to both the Belgian authorities and probably his fellow missionaries, and would lead to a parting of the ways.

CHAPTER 6
A FORGOTTEN HERO

The Foreign Office's approach to missionary involvement in the Congo reform campaign was twofold. On the one hand the missionaries kept the issue uppermost in the public mind. They could also engage public sympathy for the issue and provide a useful tool for the Foreign Office in their diplomatic efforts. The Foreign Office (FO) was aware of Danielson, and he was intended by them to play a role in the Congo campaign. The only question is whether it should be done before or after the presentation of Casement's report. The question was discussed by the directors, including F. B. Meyer and Harry Guinness, of the RBMU early in November 1903.

> [Guinness] referred to the visit he had paid to the Foreign Office where he had a prolonged conference with Lord Percy [Parliamentary Undersecretary of State] and Mr. Villiers [both dealing with Congo matters] with regard to Congo atrocities. As no difficulty on their part was raised to our publishing the facts laid before us by Mr. Danielson, it was proposed that we should make these public in January, if not earlier.[1]

Later in November, Henry Fox Bourne, the Secretary of the Aborigines' Protection Society, wrote to Morel:

> The F.O. consider (I went there yesterday) Casement's statement had better be published first, after which Danielson can follow up with more effect. It does not object to use being made of his other information – indeed would like it be done by way of keeping up public interest in the movement, which I really believe it is eager to promote.[2]

Mention is made several times in correspondence of Danielsen producing accounts of his own about what he had seen in the Congo.

For the reasons given below it shall be seen later on that that was impossible for him; however, the Foreign Office were neither against him holding public meetings nor subsequently writing about his experiences. As Morel noted to Herbert Ward, a friend of Casement,

Grattan Guinness of the CBM has some terrible information. The Foreign Office seems to desire all the pressure from public opinion they can get. Between ourselves, Farnall – the man in charge of those things at F.O. is rather pessimistic about the amount of information we are getting from Congo – said to me: "If you drop the Congo question, be sure the government will drop it."[3]

The objection lay in allowing missionaries to come too close to the official government work of the consul. Casement himself makes no direct reference to the missionaries in his report. In the documents produced by the Belgian government in answer to the Casement report 'English Protestant missionaries' are explicitly mentioned as a factor contributing to the unreliability of the evidence on which the Casement report was based. A Foreign Office memorandum was written to answer some of the charges in the Belgian *Notes*:

A visit to his countrymen was a correct proceeding on his part, and it was but natural that he should be assisted by them. As their Consul, it was right he should visit his compatriots dwelling in isolated stations amid savage surroundings… His Majesty's Government can in no way accept the view that Mr. Casement necessarily fell under the influence of missionaries…[4]

Danielsen, therefore, never received any official recognition, as stressing his involvement would only have damaged Casement's arguments.

Guinness's position shifts

Guinness must have already sensed that there was a change coming in policy towards the Congo Free State. Morel's long standing campaign was coming to fruition. Having Danielsen bring direct evidence from Casement's trip gave the CBM an insight that other missionary societies may have lacked into the seriousness of the situation in the Congo. The CBM Home Council had refused to take immediate action on Danielsen's evidence as they preferred to wait for Casement's arrival. But when Danielsen had held his first mass meetings in Edinburgh on 7th and 8th November, the attitude of the Mission began a rapid change. Morel wrote a few days after the public meetings: 'I have had a long talk with Guinness. I think the alliance established now between us will be productive of good results to all concerned.'[5] Perhaps the large audiences attracted to these meetings, or the reports of Danielsen's statements in the national press, showed the CBM Home Council that a real change in public opinion was coming about. At a board meeting on 26 November 1903 the Congo Council decided to publish a booklet of missionary

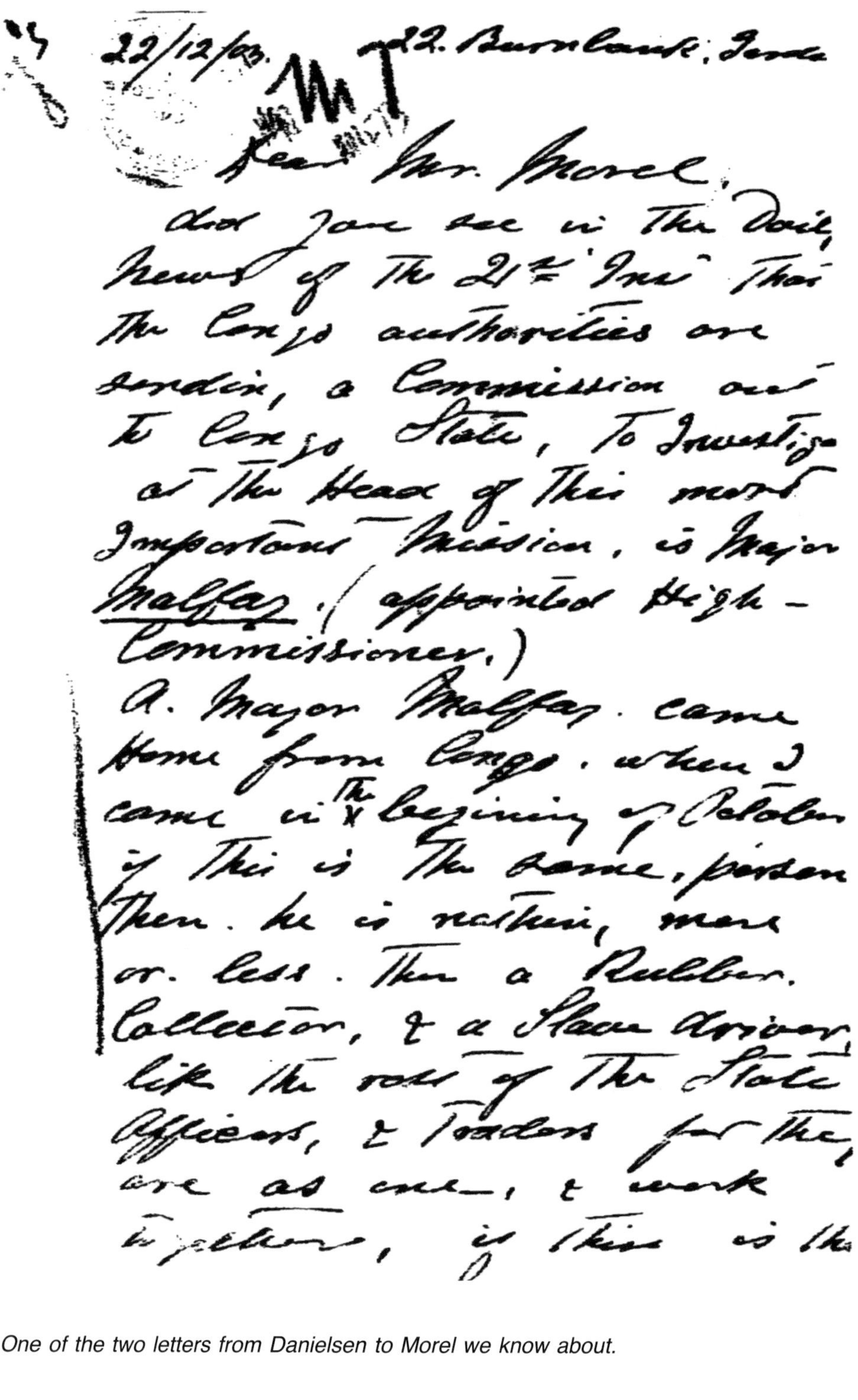

22/12/03. 22. Burnbank; Terra

Dear Mr. Morel,

Did you see in The Daily News of the 21st Inst that the Congo authorities are sending a Commission out to Congo State, to Investigate at the Head of this most Important Mission, is Major Malfaz. (appointed High-Commissioner.)

A. Major Malfaz. came Home from Congo. when I came in the beginning of October if this is the same person then. he is nothing, more or less. then a Rubber. Collector, & a Slave driver, like the rest of the State Officers, & Traders for they are as one, & work together, if this is the

One of the two letters from Danielsen to Morel we know about.

same Man?. Then is is to
send The Criminal to
Investigate into his own
Case, for to Condemn
him self. he will be sure
to Investigate very Carefully

This Major Melfor. had
been on the upper Congo
for some time,
if this is the same
Person than The World
should know how
Things stand.
yours
Sincerely.

evidence on conditions, and on 'a series of mass meetings to be held in the main cities in the UK. The Council very heartily agreed to this programme being carried out.' Guinness held the first of these, in Bristol, shortly before the arrival of Casement in England. This demonstrates a considerable change in the Mission's position. According to the letters from Morel to Danielsen, by now there was no difficulty in Morel getting the material he wanted from the CBM.[6]

Danielsen's testimony and subsequent actions demonstrably played a role in the CBM shift in position. He clearly saw the problems in the Congo and the implications of those events for his own society. His clear information and the semi-autonomous actions he took in addressing public meetings were powerful signals to the CBM board. The last known correspondence between Morel and Danielsen was on 22 December 1903 when the latter wrote to Morel about the untrustworthiness of Justin Malfeyt, the high commissioner, appointed by the Belgians to make a fresh examination of the allegations.[7] As he was a Belgian officer who had worked for the Congo Free State from 1891, and had been responsible for the handling of the complaints of the natives, Danielsen may have been be correct to assume that he was part of the establishment. With the shift in the board's position, however, Danielsen was no longer necessary as a link between the two groups. In addition, Danielsen would soon have no attention to spare for the Congo issues as he was involved in problems of his own.

Resignation

The Standing Committee letter of April 1903 had resulted in Danielsen's recall being rescinded. However this almost immediately afterwards John Harris sent a letter dated 23 June 1903 sent to the standing committee:

> With regard to Mr. Danielson's dismissal I would like to point out that the Home Council never claimed that Mr. Gilchrist's letter formed sufficient ground for their actions, and Mr. Wilkes expressly stated that the Home Council had previously almost decided to ask Mr. Danielson to resign, and you may be sure that they did not arrive at so grave a decision without having other strong reasons for their actions... let me add that the letter... whilst extolling Mr. Danielson's abilities says nothing of the manner in which he has persistently insulted some members of the Committee and Mission merely because they differed in opinion with him. So the expression "he looks well after the comfort of the passengers" might also have been added—"provided he is partial to them." Nothing has been said of the indiscretions at dealing with those outside the mission, which indiscretions might involve

the mission in trouble; for instance to call the Director of a trading company "a drunken fool" to his face might do in Denmark but not on the Congo. Mr. Danielson claims that the Standing Committee have freed him from all blame with reference to his treatment of the workers. If the Standing Committee have done that then I in company with others regret that we must disassociate ourselves from that connection … from personal observation." ALSO: "I presume Dr. Guinness expects some answer about my wife's "communication"; the facts are these: My wife said before Mr. Sawyers [sic] that she thought someone ought to communicate with the Standing Committee and call their attention to the treatment of the Steamer workers but that as she was writing to the Standing Committee re: Mr. Danielson's exorbitant charges to us she felt that if she wrote about the treatment of the men the Committee might think she wrote from prejudice.[8]

Harris obviously had a personal dislike of Danielsen. This was shared by a number of Danielsen's colleagues:

January 1904, the CBM minute book
With regard to Mr. Danielson. Letters received from Mr. Wallbaum and Mr. Steel intimating that they would be compelled to sever their connection with the CBM should he return to the Congo in the Engineering Department, and all things having been considered, it was proposed by Mr. Irvine and seconded by Mr. Jackson that the best thing would be to recommend Mr. Danielson to send in his resignation.[9]

Furthermore, on March 22 the minutes record:

A letter was read from Mr. Armstrong about Mr. Danielson and eulogising the work done of him in connection with the Engineering Department, but confirming previous reports as to his unreliability of statement. After having carefully re-considered his case it was unanimously resolved to abide by the previous decision to await report from the Field Committee in answer to Dr. Guinness's letter regarding Danielson before coming to any definite decision as to the future connection with the Mission.[10]

Wallbaum and Armstrong had both been present at the meeting of the Standing Committee which agreed to write the letter clearing Danielsen of earlier charges. However it can be seen even then that Danielsen had begun to alienate his colleagues. He seems to have fallen out with both Mr. and Mrs. Harris. Wallbaum and Steel were both engineers and so worked closely with

The final decision on Danielsen was taken at the mission station in Ikau.

Danielsen and Armstrong was chief of the mission at Bonginda where Danielsen was primarily based. He could have alienated all three men.

An alternative explanation may be found for the hostility of these three men. Roger Casement had spent time while writing his report based at the CBM mission station at Bonginda. Wallbaum, Steel, and Armstrong were all involved in his trips to the outlying districts. They were also all present at the Spelier incident discussed earlier. These letters were not written at the time Danielsen left the Congo. They were written later when the Belgian government was beginning its campaign to discredit Casement and his report. This response would have played out in the Congo Free State as well as in Europe. Already local officials had been called on to further investigate cases that Casement had been interested in. We know Armstrong had met with at least one of them.[11] Danielsen may have become politically inconvient to local CBM missionaries.

Just as the Home Council was formulating its response to the situation in the Congo, so were the missionaries in the field. The Standing Committee in Congo held a meeting on 12 and 13 May 1904.[12] Present were: W. D. Armstrong (chairman) and the CBM missionaries, Messr Ruskin, Ellery, Harris, Whiteside, Wallbaum, and Bond. The last item on the agenda was:

19. Mr. Danielson's return

Proposed by Mr. Harris, that we can as Standing Committee agree with Dr. Guinness' statement that the Home Council cannot see its way clear to send Mr. Danielson back to the field.

Seconded by Mr. Bond	(3 votes)
To the contrary	(2 votes)
Neutral	(2 votes)

The split nature of this vote shows that the missionaries themselves had no single response to the situation they found themselves in. It is interesting to explore a little the views of two very different men present in this meeting towards the events happening around them.

A parting of the ways

The internal split highlighted by the vote in May of the Standing Committee was by no means simple. The issue of Danielsen's return was not the same as making a decision on a response to the issues the missionaries faced. It is not recorded who voted in which way, which leaves us with many questions. Harris had introduced the motion: does this mean that he voted in favour of Danielsen's non-return or simply that he was the only one willing to address an unpleasant issue by proposing the motion? The minute records that Dr. Guinness had recommended that Danielsen not return; as that letter no longer exists we cannot know how strong that recommendation was. How should the neutral votes be interpreted? Were they a protest against what was viewed as an unfair decision on the part of the Home Council, or another example of the missionaries wishing not to involve themselves in a struggle they saw as political and therefore not in their purview? Also the continued references to a problem in temperament hint at some issue not fully explained. Perhaps Danielsen had argued with his colleagues before his departure. The elliptical minute will not allow any conclusions to be drawn.

An additional complication was Danielsen's desire to marry. While speaking at the Carrubber's Close mission in Edinburgh in November he had met Lina Niclasen, the daughter of Faeroese parents who were living in Leith, Edinburgh's seaport. On 17 May 1904 Danielsen had been again on the Congo Council's agenda, and this time he was pressing for a conclusion on his future within the mission, and he also informed the Council 'of his intention to get married during the coming week.'[21] After very carefully considering the matter, it was unanimously agreed that the Council could not decide anything further regarding him and his future connection with the Mission until they heard from the Field Committee in answer to the letters that had been sent out asking them for a full report. The Council did not see its way to agreeing to his immediate marriage. They felt that should the Field Committee express itself as desirous of his return there would then be time enough for them to consider the case of his fiancée. Although they could not prohibit his marriage, they felt that should it take place, it would complicate matters somewhat. The view of the Mission was understandable. Any wife was considered as a member of the staff and had therefore to be accepted by the RBMU. Danielsen, however, had as usual no patience to wait and did not take notice of the Council's opinions on the matter, and in May 1904 he married. In the event, Lina proved to be a great support of her husband, and it would certainly not have been a problem to send her to the Congo.

The fullest statement of the reasons for Danielsen's dismissal are to be found in a minute from the Home Council:

> Letters were read from members of the Field Committee with reference to Mr. Danielson's return to the field.
>
> It having been decided to take definite action on these letters instead of waiting for the Minutes of the Field committee meeting, especially as Mr. Danielson was pressing the Council for a definite answer to his future connection with the Mission.
>
> Mr. Jackson stated that in view of the fact that
>
> (i) The majority of the members of the Field Committee are opposed to his return;
>
> (ii) That should he be sent back, friction in the Engineering Department would only be perpetuated and;
>
> (iii) That he was a persona non grata with State; his service be dispensed with.
>
> The Council unanimously agreed that apart from his incompatibility of temperament there was nothing against Mr. Danielson and that if desired they would willingly recommend him as a conscientious worker, first-class mechanic and an earnest Christian.[22]

What seemed to settle the matter once and for all was Danielsen having been declared *persona non grata* by the Belgian authorities. He knew too much about what happened in the Congo. He was now known as an opponent to the rule of King Leopold II's regime, and was not afraid to impugn the king's integrity. It would also seem that Danielson, while still in the Congo, had already experienced harassment from the authorities. This is apparent from a letter that Morel had written to him shortly after Danielsen had come back to

Britain, in which Morel writes 'I have not heard of the case of murder which you say the State tried to fasten upon you.'[23] Unfortunately, this is the only reference to this incident. After their decision, however, the CBM resolved that they would support Danielsen wherever he could find work. The result was his return to his native Faeroe Islands, and the Mission decided to pay his fare of £10.[61] He returned to the Faroes on 25 July 1904, and the last connection with the Balolo Mission, according to the minute book 15 June 1905, is as follows:

> The 119th Meeting of the Congo Council held at Harley House Thursday June 15th 1905.
>
> Harry Guinness in the chair.
>
> A letter from Mr. Danielson asking the council for a recommendation, especially with reference to the Christian work he took part in while connected with the Mission, was then laid before the Council, who readily acceded to his request.

Danielsen's resignation and return to the Faroes meant that he did not take part in any further campaigning. Nevertheless, he had provided the crucial link between the reformers and the missionaries. When this group came together they would challenge the status quo in the Congo and bring Leopold's rule there to an end. However, with Danielsen passing out of active involvement, and with the severance of his links with the CBM, his founding role in the campaign would be written out of history.

CHAPTER 7
CONGO REFORM ASSOCIATION

In February 1904 Casement finished his report on Congo, which was published by the British government. It caused an international storm, not least in Belgium, where the detailed and comprehensive accounts of atrocity caused panic in the ranks of Leopold's supporters. Although Casement was pleased with the progress of campaigning, he realised that this campaign needed a greater level of organisation.

On 25 January 1904 he wrote to Morel, and referred to a letter he had written some days earlier. He had been 'suggesting the formation of a Congo Reform Committee, and the more I think of it the more vitally necessary does the creation of such body appear to be. After writing to you, I wrote in somewhat similar terms to Grattan Guinness.':

> Grattan Guinness's meetings will help it on immensely – but there, I could write it all day and I would only end with the same suggestion – get a Congo Reform Committee started – make its home Liverpool – and you will end, I believe, by making all England its membership.[1]

Casement's attitude was much friendlier towards the missionaries, perhaps unsurprisingly, given his previous experience. Morel went to Ireland to discuss the matter with Casement. Casement could not be openly associated with a lobby group, but he sent Morel £100 (equivalent of some £8,500 at present) to help the organisation get started.

> I was able to inform Casement three weeks later that a 'Congo Reform Association' was in being, with Earl Beauchamp as President, and a preliminary Committee...
>
> Dr. Guinness who at that time was waging war against King Leopold, offered to come to organise a demonstration in Liverpool if the expenses of hiring a hall could be defrayed. This was made possible by Mr. John Holt's generosity. The demonstration took place on 23 March 1904 with Mr. Alfred Emmott in the chair, supported by others. On that occasion I announced the formation of an Association and read out a long list of supporters.

The formation of the Association had cost exactly £30. Casement would not allow the balance to be refunded to him, and it formed the nucleus of the funds of the new organisation.[2]

Membership of the Congo Reform Association could be obtained on the payment of ten shillings yearly, this sum to include the regular monthly delivery, postage free, of the Journal of the Association.

As the organisation began to coalesce it led to some interesting (and sometimes uncomfortable) alliances between the humanitarians and the missionaries. In some cases humanitarians such as Morel had a low opinion of missionaries and the missionary task, but felt obliged to make use of the information (both textual and photographic) that missionaries were able and willing to provide. Yet as we shall see in the terms of the development of the CRA, the alliance remained one of convenience, rather than mutual affection.[3]

The CRA started a campaign throughout the UK and the US. At the beginning of 1904 the RBMU published a booklet, written by Harry Grattan Guinness, *Congo Slavery: A Brief Survey of the Congo Question from a Humanitarian Point of View*. The booklet consists of six parts giving a comprehensive report of the involvement of the CBM in the Congo Reform Movement. Guinness in addition gave illustrated lectures entitled 'A Reign of Terror on the Congo'. In America he personally presented the case against the administration of the Congo to President Theodore Roosevelt in 1907.[4] The CRA held hundreds of meetings at which photographs of the Congo atrocities were displayed and which had a great effect on their audiences.[5] The result of this campaign was increasing pressure on King Leopold to give up his sovereignty over the Congo. In 1908 he finally relented, and the Congo became the responsibility of the Belgian state. The situation in the Congo changed gradually and in 1913 the CRA found the improvement sufficient to warrant disbanding the organisation.[6]

The American CRA

Although Morel had supporters throughout Europe, only in the United States did the cause of Congo reform become as full-scale a crusade as it was in Britain. In September 1904, at the invitation of a group of American Congo missionaries who were already denouncing the King's rule, Morel crossed the Atlantic. He was received by President Theodore Roosevelt at the White House. He spoke at a human rights conference in Boston and urged his allies to found an American Congo Reform Association.

Mark Twain's pamphlet King Leopold's Soliloquy *made the montage famous.*

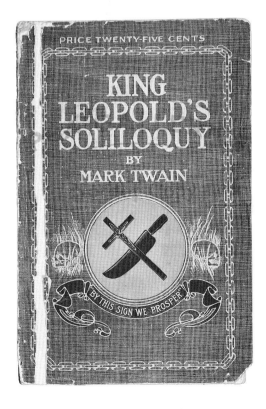

From the beginning the American campaign was livelier and more radical than the British campaign. The American association excited much interest and attracted many important supporters. Booker T. Washington, a leader in the African American community who had been born into slavery and whose recently published autobiography was entitled *Up from Slavery* (1901), was one of the vice-presidents of the association. Probably the most active celebrity member of the campaign was Mark Twain. Encouraged by Morel, Washington and Twain both spoke about Congo reform at public meetings. Deeply moved by the issue, Twain three times went to the nation's capital to lobby. In Twain the American association had found a champion every bit as press savvy as Morel, and considerably less respectful of European monarchy. *King Leopold's Soliloquy*, written by Twain in 1905, was a pamphlet in the traditions of political satire. It took the form of an imaginary dramatic monologue by Leopold. The pamphlet was radical for its time, ridiculing Leopold as a mercenary. The monologue focuses on Leopold's media campaign: 'In these twenty years I have spent millions to keep the Press of the two hemispheres quiet, and still these leaks keep occurring,'[7] says Twain's exasperated king, who rages against 'the incorruptible kodak… The only witness I have encountered in my long experience that I couldn't bribe.'[8] The pamphlet was very popular and went through two editions with all the proceeds being donated to the campaign.

Leopold always countered his opponents in the press. In the USA one of his most important agents was the lawyer Henry Kowalsky. This San Francisco attorney had been at Leopold's court for some time, employed as a lobbyist to the US government to represent the Congo Free State favourably. However, he was now sent to the USA to answer the charges against Leopold's regime.

Kowalsky had never been entirely reliable at Leopold's court, and there were jealousies among Belgian officials regarding his position. Soon various voices at court were speaking against him. The king fell prey to the atmosphere of mistrust, and Kowalsky was fired. Although he was pensioned off, the humiliated Kowalsky sold to the American newspaper magnate, Randolph Hearst, all the correspondence he had received from Leopold. The ensuing scandal was widespread and allowed the American papers to reprint details of the accusations against Leopold's Congo regime along with the missionary pictures.[9] Also included were missionary reports of events ongoing in the Congo.[10] The scandal not only affected the American public but also the government. As details of Leopold's lobbying were printed, the American government began to call for an enquiry into the Congo Free State. It proved to be a disaster for the Leopold's personal rule, leading to joint efforts from Britain and the USA to end his rule in the Congo: 'Leopold had just seen his ship of state's bowsprit blasted off by one of San Francisco's finest scoundrels.'[11]

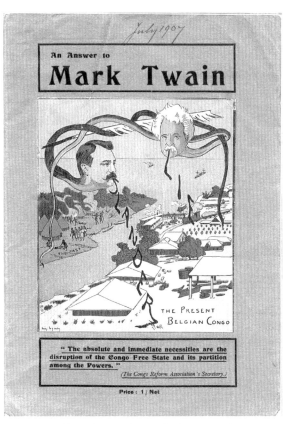

This pamphlet tries to discredit the campaign against Leopold's Congo administration.

Countering the Images

The Belgians recognised the influenced exerted by the photographs, and took action to counter them publicly. In 1907 a pamphlet was published called; *An Answer to Mark Twain*.[12] The pamphlet reprinted evidence which the Belgian government had gathered as a counter to African testimony in the Casement report. It contains sixty-three photographs showing a developing country with jobs, schools and hospitals, and a happy population.

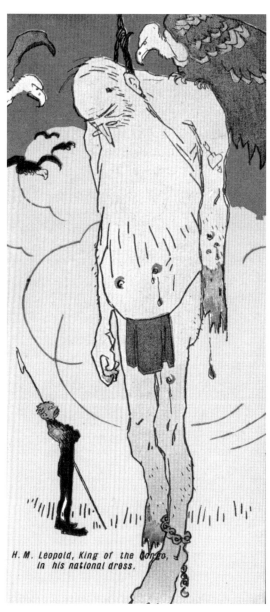

H.M. Leopold, King of the Congo, in his national dress.

Cartoon from 1908.

To look particularly at the case of Epondo, one of the most famous victims of the cut-hands (discussed below on pp.101–2), the Belgian pamphlet categorically states: 'It has now been ascertained without a shadow of a doubt, that this case is the result of a hunting accident'.[13] Soon after Casement had been in the area M. Gennaro Bosco, Acting Public Prosecutor, heard of the accusations and carried out an investigation into Epondo's case.[14] Interestingly the first criticism made of Casement's investigation is the circumstances he heard evidence in. 'From all quarters accusers appeared, and the excited crowd gave vent to all manner of accusations'.[15] The Belgians make a virtue of their own method of investigation '[the] Acting Public Prosecutor proceeded to the spot and held a judicial enquiry under the normal circumstances free from outside influences.'[16] In fact the limitation of the Belgian method is evident in Bosco's report. In the course of his investigation he heard further accusations, against the sentry Kelengo, of murder brought before the police lieutenant. When he tries to find any witness to testify on either matter '[the witnesses] took to flight and all efforts to find them have been fruitless'.[17] Both the Belgians and Casement admit the limitations of their own methods and there is no way at this distance to prove any absolute truth. The Belgian argument is that the Africans are lazy and wish to shirk work. In some ways the trump card for the Belgians is a statement from W. D. Armstrong when Epondo's case was being investigated '[that the natives are] capable of any plot to escape work and especially the labour of collecting rubber.'[18]

All of Casement's testimonies were similarly attacked, and the difficulty of establishing the absolute truth was skilfully exploited. For example, *An Answer to Mark Twain* states: 'The native represented with the two hands cut off, called Mola in the Report of the Commission of Enquiry, lost his two hands as a result of wounds on his wrist which gangrened.' However, this account of Mola's maiming looks like manipulation as the *Report of the Commission of Enquiry* had also stated: 'Mola had been captured by the soldiers. The cord with which he had been bound was too tight, causing gangrene to set in; he lost both hands.' The report had thus admitted that the mutilation had been caused by soldiers of the state. The interesting point is that the Belgian writer of *An Answer to Mark Twain* felt the need to provide such a partial account in public as a counter to the persuasive visual evidence of the atrocity photographs.

Commission of Enquiry

Leopold had established a commission after Casement's report was published in 1904 to look into its accusations. This course of action had previously been successful in pacifying public opinion. *Regions Beyond* wrote about the commission and the CBM missionaries involvement in it. In January Grattan Guinness wrote 'it is a great triumph for the movement of Congo Reform that the King of the Belgians should have appointed a special Commission to investigate the present condition of the Upper Congo in regards to the complaints now familiar to our readers.' But he was sceptical of the committee of investigation:

> It is only to be regretted that the composition of this Commission should not have been of an international, independent character. As it is, the three members constituting the commission are chosen, appointed and paid by the King, and

one cannot but recognize in these facts the comparatively unsatisfactory nature of the whole investigation... the commission can hardly report unfavourably on the system which is in reality responsible for the miseries we deplore.[19]

In March, *Regions Beyond* could report, that the commission of enquiry had been at Baringa, where the Harrises were stationed. The sceptical attitude had changed:

We are glad to note that the opinion of our missionaries at Baringa with regard to the composition of the Commission is much more favourable than we had anticipated. We hardly think better or fairer men could have been chosen than Mr. Janssen, Baron Nisco and Dr. Schumacher.[20]

The enquiry lasted three days and Harris occupied the first three sessions in addressing the commission from notes drawn by up himself and Stannard, another CBM missionary. He described the outrages, murders, cannibalism, and imprisonment that had occurred during 1904. There was so much to report that it would have taken months to get testimonies. The commission therefore agreed to accept the following, rather extraordinary, statement as true: 'That hundreds of people had been killed in this district alone for rubber, and that I could prove it by multitudes of witnesses.'[21]

The director of the Anglo-Belgian India Rubber Company (ABIR), Monsieur Longtain, was present at this stage of the proceedings. When asked if he wished to contest the statement he replied: 'No I do not wish to contest Mr. Harris's evidence. I am aware these murders have taken place.'[22] The president asked him if he understood that if he did not contest the evidence, it would stand written against the ABIR, and so he assented. Harris was at once on his feet and said there was no need for further proof, and 'that we missionaries who had been branded as liars would stand forth as exponents of the truth'.[23]

The report was at last published in November 1905, after an eight-month wait and *Regions Beyond* reported in December:

While the Commission admitted the truth of the charges brought against the Congo State – the appropriation of the land and the labour of the people, as well as the tremendous burden of taxation under which they groan – it does not give "the full and complete manifestation of the truth" it was instructed to obtain, nor even the facts that were brought before it by a multitude of witnesses. Once more King Leopold has been weighed in the balances and found wanting – will Europe once more decline to interfere?[24]

Telephone - 6065 WEST.　　　　　Telegrams—"UNYOKE," LONDON.

═══ GREAT ═══
Congo Demonstration

THE PROTEST OF CHRISTIAN ENGLAND,

IN THE

ROYAL ALBERT HALL,

(Three minutes' walk from either High Street, Kensington, or South Kensington Stations, District Rly.
Omnibuses from all parts of London pass the door).

Friday, November 19th, 1909, at 7.30 p.m.

SPEAKERS:

His Grace THE ARCHBISHOP OF CANTERBURY.

Rev. JOHN CLIFFORD, M.A., D.D.

The Right Rev. THE LORD BISHOP OF LONDON.

Rev. J. SCOTT LIDGETT, M.A., D.D.

The Right Rev. THE LORD BISHOP OF OXFORD.

Rev. C. SILVESTER HORNE, M.A.

**Supported by a large body of Bishops, Clergy and Ministers of
all denominations.**

RESERVED SEAT TICKETS, PRICE 5/-, 2/6, 1/-

A portion of the Hall has been set aside for **Free Reserved Seat
Tickets,** which may be obtained by enclosing a penny stamp to—
TRAVERS BUXTON, Esq., at address as below.

FUNDS towards the cost of this Demonstration are
URGENTLY NEEDED and will be thankfully received and acknowledged by
TRAVERS BUXTON, Esq.,
51, Denison House, Vauxhall Bridge Road,
London, S.W.

*As late as 1909 there were demonstrations against the administration in the Congo. This
one was organised by John Harris and Edward Talbot, Bishop of Southwark.*

Arthur Conan Doyle, who had also become involved in the CRA campaign, concluded in the long pamphlet that he wrote in 1909, *The Crime of the Congo*, that 'the effect of that Report, when stripped of its courtly phrases, was an absolute confirmation of all that had been said by so many witnesses during so many years. It is easy to blame the Commissioners for not having the full courage of their convictions, but their position was full of difficulty.'[25]

The results of the commission were an unmitigated disaster for Leopold. He had meant this to be another lame committee to quieten criticism. Instead, the Commission came back with a damning report, confirming almost all the charges Morel and others had made. Paul Costermans, the territory's acting governor, committed suicide after the report's publication. News surfaced that one of the judges, while listening to a succession of witnesses, had broken down and wept.[26] The actual transcripts of the 300, mostly African, witnesses interviewed were withheld until the 1980s.[27] The report signalled an end to Leopold's rule. The Belgian government annexed the Congo Free State in 1908.

Strained Relations

On Friday, 19 November 1909, a great Congo Demonstration was held in the Royal Albert Hall in London. This was 'the protest of Christian England', which was to be supported by a large body of bishops, clergy and ministers of all denominations. *Regions Beyond* carried advertisements for the meeting, and in December had a report from it. The report appeared under the headline 'What Britain Demands'. It describes the emotion of people as late as in 1909:

It is a stirring spectacle that is witnessed in the interior of the Royal Albert Hall on the evening of Friday November 19th, as a vast multitude assembles in the subdued light, under the spell of the organ music, to record their united protest on behalf of the oppressed races of Congo-land. Presently the lights go up, and now the whole assembly are on their feet and loudly cheering as a procession of brilliant ecclesiastics comes into view, with the Bishop of London and Dr. Clifford conversing at its head, and behind them the Archbishop of Canterbury in company with other denomination leaders. Certainly it is no ordinary occasion that has brought together so representative a group of speakers. And now the Archbishop, who has come to preside over this assembly of Christian England, introduces the business of the evening in a speech which is deliberate, weighty, and illuminating, and which evidently has the hearty and emphatic support of the distinguished company who is throng the platform. Then follow Dr. Clifford, with fireworks which starts the echoes; the Bishop of Oxford with a merciless exposure which extorts the laughter of the audience; the Rev. C. Silvester Horne, the grace and fire of whose ringing oratory thrills and moves and masters those who listen, and the Rev. J. Scott Lidgett, who handles a difficult aspect of the situation with statesmanlike skill. Then the Bishop of London, who knows both his subject and his audience, skilful and yet emphatically gives the summing up. His statement of "British Demands" is clear and unwavering. Nor does he forget a well-merited tribute to Rev. J.H. Harris, to whose untiring efforts the success of the great meeting is largely due...

In conclusion the vast audience rise to their feet to declare the approval of the following resolution:

"That the Meeting, Remembering the special responsibilities by the people and Government of this country in the events which lead to the creation of the Congo Free State, and recalling the participation of Great Britain in the Berlin Conference of 1885; And believing that no greater can threaten a Christian nation than failure to abide by the moral obligations it has deliberately contracted; Declare that as long as the cruel oppression under which, in violation alike of the principles of humanity and of definite Treaty obligations, the natives of the Congo have long been suffering, is maintained, the people of Great Britain are bound to press forward unflinchingly their demand for a complete reform of the whole system of administration in the Congo territory," and with the singing of the National Anthem a historic meeting ends.[28]

The meeting in 1909 was both a high point of support for the Congo reform campaign and a recognition of the huge victory already achieved; the end of Leopold's personal rule over the territory. This success should not be underplayed. One of the first human rights campaigns of modern times had, through careful use of evidence, forced a government out of power. Not a single shot had to be fired in Europe but the Belgians were forced to bow to public pressure.

After Leopold's personal rule had ended Morel had a serious disagreement with the CBM over their acceptance of new sites in the Congo from the Belgian authorities:

Attention was called to an article on the Congo Balolo Mission written by Mr. Morel and published in the Official Organ of the Congo Reform Association. The opinion was expressed that Mr. Morel had gone out of his way to insult the Congo Council. After due consideration the Secretary was directed to write Mr.

Morel a judicious letter, informing him that they felt very much hurt by his remarks and point out that the apparently friendly attitude of Belgian & Congo officials to Dr. Guinness and our missionaries leads the Congo Council to hope that a change for the better in the administration of the Congo will soon take place.[29]

The CBM interpreted increased friendliness towards the mission as a sign that the Belgian government really intended to make changes for the better in the system of administration in the Congo. Morel had regarded it as a bribe to obtain their silence. For a time the matter blew over but after annexation Morel could not count on the support of the CBM. As the formal campaign was wound down, the loose ties which had bound this disparate group of reformers disintegrated completely.

In the December number of 1908, *Regions Beyond* told its readers:

On November 11th, 1908, the Congo Free State passed out of existence. Let us record the fact with thanksgiving, as the first decisive victory in an unfinished campaign. King Leopold retires, having duly decorated his satellites, and now to Belgium falls the task of reshaping the aftermath. On the Congo, how much is hoped for this change. There, the news of annexation has been hailed with delight, by those long weary of watching torture and death. The groanings occasioned by forced labour still reach our missionaries' ears; the natives still come with their pitiful tales… Let us remember them until they [the atrocities] cease; until the Congo administration has been completely reversed and the spirit of liberty and humanity transforms that fetid air. No more substitution of one government for another can accomplish this change. There must be a determined vigilance on the natives; a resolute enquiry into Belgium's intention and plans; an instance that natives rights in land and produce shall be respected, freedom of trade secured and forced labour abolished.[30]

In 1909, Guinness was telling the CBM council with satisfaction:

Speaking to an exceedingly intelligent native at Stanley Pool the other day I asked him with regard to recent changes at Leopoldville. His reply was unhesitating: "The old bad times are past. To-day we are free!" Needless to say, this testimony does not yet apply to the whole Congo, but the practical trend of events in the right direction we can afford to be both thankful and hopeful.[31]

On 16 June 1913, the CRA held its final meeting at the Westminster Palace Hotel in London. Many of the British supporters of the case were together for the last time or sent letters or telegrams of support that were read aloud. A series of distinguished speakers praised Morel. Morel seldom liked sharing too much of the limelight, but when he replied on this occasion he gave the greatest credit to someone else: 'While I was listening to all that was being said, I had a vision. The vision of a small steamer ploughing

The last meeting of Congo Reform Association was held at Westminster Palace Hotel in London.

in way up the Congo just 10 years ago this month, and on its decks a man that some of you know, at man of great heart ... Roger Casement.'[32] Of course that vision of a steamer rightly has Danielsen at its helm.

This is how the artist has imagined the positions of the heroes of this story on board Henry Reed *while sailing along the Congo River.*

Lasting good?

Adam Hochschild poses an important question: did the CRA bring about any lasting good? Hochschild notes that reports of abuses against wild rubber gatherers declined and that hostage taking and officially sanctioned severing of hands also became much rarer.[33] However Hochschild does not attribute these gains to the effort of the reformers. Instead he believes that outside forces such as the shift from wild to synthetic rubber brought about change in the Congo. For Hochschild any gains made by the CRA were felt solely in Europe where a new form of humanitarian enterprise had been discovered and made successful.[34]

Dean Pavlakis finds Hochschild too pessimistic. Morel and the other reformers felt that a great many of their aims had been fulfilled:

„The reports from the Congo tracked overall improvement. Within a year of annexation, before the major reforms, atrocities diminished, suggesting improved accountability and control under Belgian rule. In October 1910, Acting Consul Gerald Campbell, hitherto a severe critic of Belgian rule, reported, with a few exceptions missionaries and traders alike report that the treatment which the natives in the interior are receiving at the hands of the State officials has perceptibly improved. These reports have been received since the reform decrees came into force on the 1st July last…; enquiries are, moreover, being held into such occurrences as have come to the knowledge of the Government. There are signs that the former regime… is undergoing a radical change, and that it is the wish of the Government that the new decrees which aim at the betterment of the condition of the natives shall be sincerely interpreted".[35]

Of course the CRA's leadership still had reservations with regards to the Belgian colonial authorities' intentions. Issues remained surrounding land rights, governance, and forced labour. The Belgian Congo remained under a colonial administration however the violence which had marred the Congo Free State to a large extent receded. In May 1911, Consul Mackie observed 'there is substantial ground for the belief that crime and oppression are now the exception and not the rule'.[36]

It can therefore be concluded that the campaigns of the CRA made a lasting impact both on Western public consciousness but also on the lives of the Africans on whose behalf the campaign was fought. Danielsen and the others who came after him really did manage to put an end to the violence meted out in the Congo Free State.

CHAPTER 8

EVANGELICALS, ATROCITY PHOTOGRAPHS, AND DANIELSEN

In the late nineteenth and early twentieth century's, European missionaries took thousands of photographs to be viewed by an audience at home. The missionary photographs from the Congo made a sizeable impact on the European and American public consciousness. The campaign for reform in the Congo is one of the first places that an articulation of the modern-day doctrine of human rights appears in a recognisable form. One of the distinct features of the campaign was the widespread use of photographs to communicate its message. According to Sharon Sliwinski, these two facts are no coincidence, and she argues that '[the] very recognition of what we call human rights is inextricably bound to a particular kind of aesthetic encounter. Historical inquiry into the Con-

'The Lantern, through which distant places and peoples are brought near to our helpers, with its operator, Mr. Sambridge.'

go reform movement shows that the conception of rights did not emerge from the articulation of an inalienable human dignity, but from a particular visual encounter with atrocity.'[1]

Many of the photographs which survive from the period are kept in an archive at Anti-Slavery International in London.[2] Details of the photographs are scarce. Most photographs have been taken by missionaries but no records were ever made of photographer's name, subject's name, date or the location. This chapter will make various claims about the missionary photographs. Firstly, that a group of them must have been taken during Casement's journey as evidence for his claims. Secondly, that the famous 'cut-hands' photographs most likely were part of the group taken during Casement's journey. Thirdly, that Daniel J. Danielsen was the photographer of at least some of these photographs.

The 'cut-hand' photographs

The cut-hand photographs which would become so closely associated with the CRA campaigns had a particular format. Usually of a lone male figure with the severed or mutilated limb held against a length of white cloth tied sarong-like around the waist. The cloth serves two purposes: first it provides a vivid backdrop for the foregrounding of the 'atrocity' wound; and secondly it provides a modest covering to suit the sensibilities of the Edwardian audiences for which it was intended. These photographs are posed by their photographers for the sake of those who look at them later as evidence of atrocities. They are not an attempt to record the people present in them but an attempt to show their victimhood. David van Reybrouck points to the irony that the number of people with cut hands was not as high as the number of people killed, but photographs showing mutilations had a greater impact than reports of the dead.[3]

The first photograph published which belongs in this series was in 1902 in E. D. Morel's *Affairs of West Africa*.[4] Previous writers on the topic of the Congo atrocity photographs have placed them and their use later, but this image places them earlier. It also shows that the composition that was used in the most famous of the images had already been developed as early as 1902.

A chapter in *Affairs of West Africa* was given over to describing the excesses of the system of forced labour at work in the Congo,[5] and the accompanying picture is printed purely for its visual impact. No name or story is printed along with the picture to identify the subject.[6] We can say with some confidence however that this photograph was of a boy called Yoka because the boy was photographed again along with Mola Ekulite. Casement met Ekulite at

Ikoko in an ABMU missionary station.[7] In the earlier picture of Yoka the boy perches on the edge of a chair. He wears the white length of cloth but also a tunic top. The arm is in this case held up to be more easily visible however it is the left hand which comes across more clearly held against the white cloth.

There is no history of the boy in the photograph printed to tell us how he came to be hurt or what happened to him after these two photographs were taken. It is possible that the photographer was an ABMU missionary. Both Morel and Casement had close links with their field missionaries. Morel published or republished evidence by the Swedish ABMU missionary, Sjöblom, and also Joseph Clark.[8] He admired William Morrison greatly, but it is unlikely he was the photographer as he worked in another area of the country. Casement and Clark were close friends, and Casement visited Ikoko during his trip on the Congo. The ABMU was also the missionary society which supplied Casement with the steamer for his trip up the river.

The first photographs taken during Casement's 1903 trip which can be dated were taken at Ikoko. It is therefore significant that someone there had already taken a cut-hand photograph and that photograph had been published to provide evidence of atrocity and provoke outrage. A missionary at Ikoko knew the potential of these photographs and had already formulated a visual framework for them.

The Montage

The most famous images from the campaign are those in the montage of nine photographs of mutilated persons (see p. 100). These appeared in the second edition of Mark Twain's pamphlet *King Leopold's Soliloquy*.

The montage also illustrated the front page of the first edition of Sir Arthur Conan Doyle's *The Crime of the Congo*, published in 1909. Conan Doyle was Morel's most significant new recruit after 1908 to the cause of Congo reform. In his book, based on Morel's material, Conan Doyle called the exploitation of the Congo 'the greatest crime which has ever committed in the history of the world.'[9] The photograph montage reproduced in both books is easily found online even today. But in the most cases no photographer is mentioned, nor are the victims identified.

Nobody seems to have recorded the history which we have for the people in the montage. Here is an attempt. It is probable that at least five of the nine photographs date from Casement's stay at the ABMU station in Ikoko and at least three of the other photographs were taken during his stay at the CBM station at Bonginda.[10] It looks quite clear that those photographs on the montage are from the same collection with the same backdrop and posture which

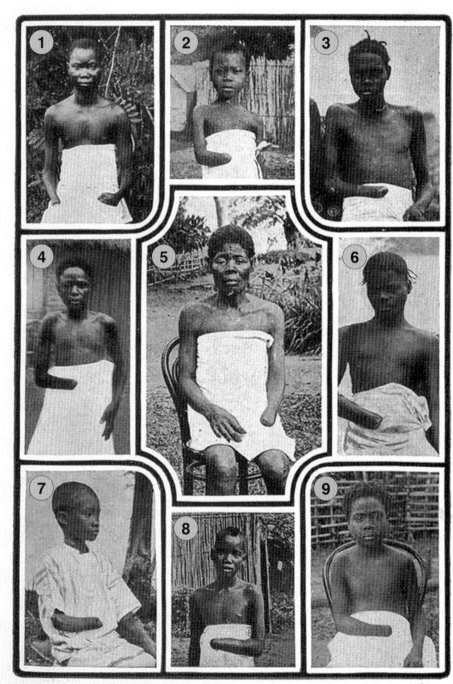

FROM PHOTOGRAPHS, CONGO STATE

These photographs can be identified as follows:

1. *Mola Ekulite, Ikoko*
2. *Lokoto, Bonginda*
3. *Man from Ikoko*
4. *Ikabo, Bonginda*
5. *Woman, probably from Ikoko.*

6. *Man from Ikoko*
7. *Boy unknown*
8. *Epondo, Bonginda*
9. *Boy probably from Ikoko*

has been used in Ikoko. In addition, the manner in which the cloth is tied is similar in each photograph. Therefore, it is very likely, that the same photographer has taken all these photographs, and it can only be Danielsen, as he was the only westerner with Casement in both Bonginda and Ikoko.[11]

In Casement's report at least four of the victims have a history and following is a summary:

Epondo, Bonginda

A lad, about 14 or 15 years of age, Epondo by name, whose left had been cut off, the stump wrapped up in a rag, the wound being yet scarcely healed, appears, and in answer to Consul's question charges a sentry named "with having done it."

Consul questions Epondo: "How long ago was it your hand was cut off?"

Answer: "He is not sure."

Two fellow villagers – young men – step out and state, that they remember. The act occurred when the clay was being dug over on the mission beach at Bonginda, when the slip place for the steamers was began.

Mr. Danielson here states that the work referred to, when the cutting for the Mission Slip was begun, was started on the 21st January of this year.[12]

W.D. Armstrong with some men from the neighbourhood of Bonginda.

101

Ikabo, Bonginda

Ikabo's hand had been cut off by a sentry of La Lulanga Company, who was, or had been quartered there. This sentry at the time he had mutilated Ikabo, had also shot dead one of the chief men of the town. Ikabo, in addition to this mutilation, had been shot in the shoulder blade, and, as a consequence, was deformed. On being shot it was said he had fallen down insensible, and the sentry had then cut off his hand, alleging that he would take it [the hand] to the Director of the Company.

Lokoto, Bonginda

Lokoto was from Mpelenge, which lies within 3 miles from Bonginda. Some years ago Mpelenge had been attacked by several sentries of the Lulanga Company. This was owing to their failure in supplying a sufficiency of india-rubber. The chief of the sentries Mokwolo had knocked down Lokoto with the butt of his gun and had then cut off his hand.[13]

Mola Ekulite, Ikoko

I found this man in the Mission Station at Ikoko on the 29th July, and learned that he had been kept by the missionaries for some years, since the day when a party of native teachers had found him in his own town some miles away from Ikoko. Mola's statement was as follows:

State soldiers came from Bikoro, and attached the Bwanga town, which they burned, killing people. They then attacked a town called Mauto, killing people there also. From that they went on to Mokili. The Mokili people fled into the forest, leaving some of their number behind with food to offer to the soldiers – among whom was Mola.

The soldiers took prisoners all the men left in the town and tied them up. Their hands were tied very tight with native rope, and

This photograph was first printed in Morel's book Affairs of West Africa *from 1902. It is likely that it shows Yoka. The photographer was probably a missionary at one of the American Baptist Missionary Union Stations.*

they were tied outside in the open; and it was raining very hard. Their hands swelled, because the tong contracted. Mola's hands had swollen terribly in the morning, and the thongs had cut into the bone.

The soldiers seeing this beat his hands against a tree with their rifles, and he was released. His hands subsequently fell off or sloughed away.

Afterwards some boys from the mission came to preach at Mokili, and they found him without his hands, and later on he came to the mission, where he has since been maintained by Mr. Clark, the leader of the mission in Ikoko.[14]

The images in the montage seem to be closely tied to Casement and his journey through the Congo; the photographer must have worked and travelled with Casement. Kevin Grant writes

But, one may ask, why did not Armstrong or other missionaries distribute "atrocity photos" earlier? It is possible that this was a new idea proposed by Casement, but it is also likely that Armstrong came upon the idea while watching Casement interpret the mutilated bodies of Africans as decisive proof of the state's brutality.[15]

Armstrong and Harris

The missionary contribution to the Congo Reform campaign has been relatively less well explored than that of secular reformers.[16] There has been a tendency amongst historians to mention only those names which were well-known within the missionary movement. The name most connected with the

John and Alice Harris.

early atrocity photographs has been the Revd William Armstrong, who was mission head at the CBM station in Bonginda.[17]

Armstrong is mentioned in passing in Casement's diary in a reference which evidently refers to a photograph being taken: 'Lokola (also named Lokoto) of Mpelenge, 3 miles from Bonginda. Taken by Revd. W. D. Armstrong of C.B.M at Bonginda on 27 August 1903.'[18] Armstrong is also positively named by Morel in *King Leopold's Rule* as a source for some of the photographs reproduced there.[19]

That Armstrong makes a likely candidate as photographer is also due to his proximity to Casement during his journey in the Congo. A number of the young men, who can be identified in the pictures we have, can only be recognised because they were used as witnesses in the Casement Report. Although their testimony is recorded, Casement did not use photographs in his report.[20] The similarity in *all* these photographs suggest that they were taken by the same person as there was a set of visual principles guiding the set-up of the images.[21] From the lack of a direct link to Casement in the dissemination of the photographs, another person can be detected in their existence.[22]

Nsala looking at the mutilated hand and foot of his daughter. This is the first known atrocity photograph by Alice Harris taken in May 1904.

Armstrong, therefore, is a strong candidate for photographer. But there are some problems in this attribution. Firstly, Armstrong was not in Ikoko with Casement when the first photographs which we know about were taken.

A case can also be made that Armstrong was not sympathetic to the kind of ideas which the Casement report embodied. W. D. Armstrong later wrote a history of the early years of the CBM which exists in manuscript.[23] In it the first ten years of the mission are meticulously detailed. The text dwells on the many dangers faced by the early missionaries. Not only were the people hostile, but the climate itself caused many deaths. Each missionary's death is covered in detail. The experience of such loss must have had a profound experience on any western missionary who witnessed it. Armstrong shows sympathy towards the Belgians, describing the urbanity of one of the local officials he befriended, and praising the comfort that the new railway line brought to travel in the Congo. A great deal of Armstrong's coverage of African society focuses on the battles that many missionaries felt they were fighting with African witch doctors. These tales contained part of the justification for the missionary enterprise. Missionaries believed they were in Africa to save the Africans from the savagery of their own societies. Armstrong certainly adhered to this view. His interpretation of the rubber system was therefore different to Casement's analysis. Armstrong calls the system a 'return to barbarism' focusing on the fact that much of the actual violence was committed by African overseers. Armstrong interpreted the whole as a return to the brutal society which had existed before the Europeans arrived. Perhaps most tellingly, while each missionary's death is detailed in his manuscript over an entire chapter, the whole of the Casement report and its aftermath is given only two paragraphs, and the narrative

From the West African Mail, 26th February 1904. The caption states that this is a 'Swedish missionary' and it was taken 'last autumn'. But as this dating corresponds with Casement's expedition, it is one more indication that this is in fact Danielsen.

swiftly moves on to the much more important arrival of a new mission printing press in 1903.

We can see that Armstrong was reasonably fair-minded. He helped Casement freely while he was in Bonginda. Nevertheless, he could not agree with the political implications of the report. He did not see the same structural causes that were so apparent to Casement, and which Danielsen evidently shared, to judge from his press reports. A tendency to disassociate with any political organisations was a feature of the faith missions.[24] In 1904 Dugald Campbell, a Brethren missionary from Glasgow to what would become Northern Rhodesia, had sent home for publication accounts of ivory raiding in Katanga in eastern Congo, and of the attendant burning of villages, mutilations and deaths. In a letter from Campbell to Fox Bourne he described the reaction:

> Our friends at home and one or two of our missionaries in the field have been so annoyed at our mixing up in the Congo controversy that misunderstanding have been created and our work has suffered … As you doubtless know we are a very conservative people and averse to politics and public controversy and my speaking out has led to a petty quibble amongst ourselves.[25]

Even if Armstrong had agreed with Casement's assessment of events he may not have felt it was the place of the missionaries to interfere.

After the presentation of Casement's report, he complained to the District Commissioner that the task of delivering the foodstuff to the mission station was badly carried out. He emphasized it was due to the people's laziness. For the same reason no better dwellings had been built and no isolation huts for those suffering from sleeping sickness. The missionary went so far as to request that a 'sentinelle' be sent to compel the people of the district to build better houses. The authorities noticed at once that this was counter to Casement's ideas.[26] But David Lagergren noted in his book *Mission and State in Congo*, that Armstrong was quite friendly to the rubber company ABIR: '[Armstrong writes] We trust, that we shall long have the privilege of working alongside the ABIR, and to promote those sentiments of friendship between your company and or Mission, which have always been so cordial.'[27]

The best-known atrocity photographer is the CBM missionary Alice Harris. She was stationed, along with her husband John Harris, at Baringa, about 100 miles up the river from Bonginda. The first photograph Harris is known to have taken was in May 1904.[28] A man, Nsala, whose daughter had been killed by sentries, came to the mission station carrying the hand and foot of his daughter. Harris persuaded him to pose with the remains.

Harris's photographs would go on to be made into a magic-lantern show which would become integral to the CRA campaign for reform in the Congo. Although Alice Harris is often named as the photographer for the photographs of the actual victims posing with the stumps where their severed hands had been, her involvement is of too late a date to make her a possible candidate. She did not meet Casement on his journey in the Congo in 1903.

While John Harris did correspond with Morel prior to 1904 it seems likely that the activism of the couple, who would become extremely involved with the CRA, seems to have been triggered by the shift in attitude which the Casement Report brought about. John Harris became immediately involved with the Belgian Commission of Enquiry. Alice Harris took her first atrocity photograph in 1904, perhaps seeing for the first time that this was a subject which prompted a photograph. In 1905 John and Alice Harris returned to Britain to become the most tireless of the missionary campaigners for reform in the Congo.

Danielsen as photographer

The most relevant fact to suggest Danielsen as photographer is his proximity to Casement during his journey through the Congo. It has already been argued that most of the photographs are the work of a single person and that their origin must be closely associated with Casement's journey. Danielsen is the only missionary who was with Casement at both times

Mola Ekulite is in the centre. He lived near Ikoko. Cropped images of the men on either side appear above in the montage.

in the early part of his tour through ABMU mission stations and the later part of his tour through CBM stations. In fact he was with Casement daily from 17 July to 15 September. His complete support of Casement's cause when he returned to Britain show the impact the journey with Casement had had on him. Kevin Grant's words quoted above with regards to Armstrong fit Danielsen's later actions much better. Casement does name Armstrong as photographer for a photograph of Lokola, but this suggests the event was something out of the ordinary. If Armstrong were producing the volume of photographs which we now have why would that one be worthy of mention in particular? If Danielsen was daily taking photographs, then it would not be a special event worthy of mention.

There is one photograph of a European holding the cut-hand of a victim (see p. 105). In the Slavery International Archive this photograph is subtitled 'Swedish missionary and mutilated child'. The same photograph

A widow weeping beside her husband, shot dead by a sentry. Photographer Mr. Whiteside from the CBM.

was kept by the Danielsen family in the Faroes ever since it was brought to the islands in early March 1904 and preserved by them as a photograph of Danielsen himself.[29] The image has been blurred and so later enhanced to make it clearer. The African's face has been most heavily altered, but the European's hair has also been coloured in. It cannot be said with absolute certainty that this is Danielsen, but there is a definite resemblance. What makes the photograph interesting is what the missionary figure is doing. He is holding the arm with the missing limb in front of his very white tropical clothes to foreground the mutilation. If this is indeed Danielsen, it is further evidence of his desire to highlight the Congo atrocities.

CHAPTER 9
PICTURES IN MOTION

Although there has been solid academic work done on the uses of atrocity photographs within the CRA campaign, their very early history has not been well traced. This chapter will focus on the very early history of the photographs, beginning with the importance of the photographs in missionary magic lantern lectures. It will show that Danielsen was the first missionary to give these lectures. The second section will be a detailed look at correspondence between Morel, Danielsen, and Harry Grattan Guinness which proves that Danielsen travelled home with a number of photographs. The last section looks at the very early publication of atrocity photographs in 1904.

A Lantern in the Faroes

Many cut-hands photographs appeared in journals, newspapers and Morel's works, by far the biggest impact came through their use in magic lanterns shows.[1] Missionary societies were well aware of the power of well-organised lantern shows to attract large audiences and potentially large donations.

One of the most successful practitioners of the missionary lantern show was Dr Harry Grattan Guinness. In the late 1880s he began a series of magic lantern tours throughout Britain on a grand scale. In one week in Glasgow in the 1890s, audiences totalling almost thirty thousand had attended his lectures.[2]

Guinness began a series of lectures entitled 'A Reign of Terror on the Congo' in 1904, 'drawing thousands of people with the promise of lantern slides.'[3] Grattan Guinness's missionary lantern lectures had some of the same public appeal as a modern rock tour, with thousands of people attending a lecture, which could last for several hours and which usually included hymn singing as well as the lantern show itself.[4] Kevin Grant has described Guinness's lectures in *A Civilised Savagery*:

Guinness focused on the savagery of the Congo Free State, realizing its betrayal of humanity through the display of atrocity photographs. These photographs were contextualized with what missionaries later called "horror narratives": descriptions of the events that preceded and caused the alleged atrocity, the process through which the atrocity was committed, and the aftermath of the event. As Guinness commented to Morel: "Some of the slides are immensely effective."[5]

The Harris slide show, consisting of Alice Harris' photographs, was the most important of the magic lantern lectures on the subject. Although the Harris slide show itself is no longer extant a version produced by the Riley brothers containing some of the same photos still exists.[6] In adverts for the Harris slide show there were sixty slides advertised but only four of these would actually show victims of the atrocities. As with other speakers it was the context which speakers gave the pictures that produced the emotional effect on audiences.

Morel increasingly became uncomfortable with the emphasis missionaries put on their own evangelical ambitions in Africa while preaching the cause of Congo reform. The advert for their slide show gives a sense of why that might be so. Thirty-eight slides were devoted to 'philanthropy in the operation' which presumably refers to missionary efforts.[7] As a tool for campaigning the magic lantern slide show reached its height with the Harris's.

While the Harris slide show was famous in its own right, none of those photographs can be identified with the early atrocity photographs. Grant also writes, that 'it is not clear that Harris knew about Armstrong's atrocity photographs before Mrs. Harris took her own.'[8] This is the first atrocity photograph taken by Harris that we know about, which was taken in May 1904, and it was after that date that Alice Harris sent her first atrocity photograph to Britain.

As has already been detailed Danielsen gave his first lectures on the cause of Congo Reform in Scotland. These lectures were the first of their kind and made a modest impact in the Scottish press. In early 1904, Danielsen went back to the Faroe islands. On 9th March 1904 this announcement was made in one of the main papers in the Faroes, *Tingakrossur*:

Photographs from Africa

Tonight, Wednesday, and on Saturday at 8 p.m. the missionary D. J. Danielsen will show slides in the Club's Theatre from the Congolese state, photographs taken by himself, including maps, landscapes, different people, and events from the activities of the English missionaries and the Belgian society's work in Africa.

Admission: 25 cents, to be paid at the entrance.[9]

In the same paper the following article appeared:

An excellent show

The missionary Daniel Danielsen, who left this town approximately 15 years ago as an engineer, and who has returned home from his work in Central Africa on a short visit, will tonight and Saturday give the people from his home town the opportunity to see some series of slides showing nature and human life in the Congolese state and – most of all the behaviour of the regime of horror that is caused by the capitalistic Belgian interests in the state. As some of our readers may remember, we published an article on these horrors in August last year.[10] These horrors have for some time moved the English government to take action and through the presence of a consul whom they have appointed, obtained reliable information on this situation. Mr. Danielsen has been this consul's companion and interpreter, and he has after his return to England given several lectures on this tragic matter. On one occasion there were as many as 3000 people attending.

Mr. Danielsen's slides and lecture this evening will illustrate these facts.

Among these slides   more than 80 in total – there are some taken directly of the locals in the Congo, who have had their right hands cut off by the tyrannical Belgians and their soldiers – a commonly used means of punishing criminals over there. We hope that the well-travelled Missionary will not let this opportunity pass without talking about the barbarism of the white side that he has witnessed during his stay among the cannibals.

Such a rare and interesting evening at such a low price is a great event and we can no doubt expect to see the house filled with people.

Danielsen went from village to village with his lecture. Their dates show that he was holding his meetings in the Faroe Islands even before the Congo Reform Association had become active in Britain. The advertisement, presumably inserted by Danielsen himself, shows conclusively that he took his own photographs in the Congo. We now turn to tracing the early history of these photographs during Danielsen's return from the Congo to Britain in late 1903 and early 1904.

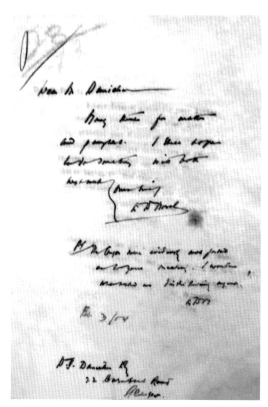

A letter of thanks from Morel to Danielsen. Morel's handwriting is not easily legible and most of his letters were typed.

The photographs' transmission

Historians have been unsure how the missionary photographs made their way to the wider public. T. Jack Thompson names Casement as the most likely carrier of the photographs.[11] However Casement arrived in England on 1 December 1903 and Danielsen's photographs were discussed and used in Britain before Casement's arrival.[12] There are clear indications, then, that the first photographs used in the Congo campaign, and also later by Guinness, came from Danielsen. In this matter, he was also ahead of others in the campaign. As has already been shown, a photograph of the cut-hands and the general composition of these images had already been established by 1902.

During the correspondence with Morel the address of Danielsen was 22 Burnbank Gardens, Glasgow.

A reappraisal of Morel's correspondence with Guinness and Danielsen shows that there is concrete evidence that Danielsen was connected to photographs from the Congo, especially the atrocity ones which Morel was anxious to acquire for his campaign. In what follows, the relevant extracts are reproduced.

Morel to Guinness, 17 November 1903:

We arranged – did we not, that in the event of you postponing publication that matter could appear on the same day in your magazine and in the West African Mail, so I trust you will therefore be so kind to let your magazine appear on the same Friday in the week, the West African Mail appearing that day … Is there any objection to my publishing one or two of his [Danielsen's] photographs before the matter comes to hand?[13]

Morel repeatedly applies to both Guinness and Danielsen to be given possession of the photographs Danielsen has brought back with him. The number of letters going back and forth suggests that the missionaries were in no hurry

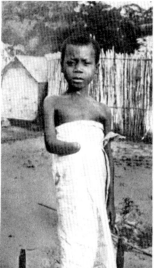
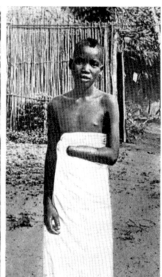

| Ikabo | Lokoto | Epondo |

Children mutilated by Congo Soldiery, all taken in Bonginda. These are the photographs from King Leopold's Rule in Africa. *Morel attributes those photographs to Armstrong, but there can be little doubt that Danielsen is the photographer. These photographs appear in the montage.*

to hand these photographs over. Note in the last sentence that the photographs are referred to definitely as Danielsen's.

Morel to Danielsen, 17 November 1903

Of course I have had conversation and correspondence with Dr. Grattan Guinness about your information. My feeling is that Government or no Government we should lose no further time in publishing the information, I think the delay weakens our case. I have told Dr. Grattan Guinness so, but each man must judge for himself. The idea now is to postpone the publication of your matter until January, when it is to appear simultaneously in the Regions Beyond journal, and the West African Mail, but I have asked Dr. Grattan Guinness if he can place some of your photographs at my disposal before that date, perhaps you will write him to the same effect?[14]

This letter of the same date is further evidence of the photographs being Danielsen's. The reference to 'your matter' was probably about a piece of writing which Danielsen would produce on his trip with Casement. This never appeared. Again Morel definitely refers to the photographs as belonging to Danielsen.

Morel to Danielsen, 26 November 1903

As you know Dr. Grattan Guinness has promised to let me have all your matter, in order to publish it simultaneously in the West African Mail and the Regions Beyond Journal whenever he decides to publish it, so I hope there will be no doubt about that being done. He also said he would let me have your photographs. If you are passing through Liverpool at any time, I hope you will come and see me. Of course you understand my feeling is that I should like your stuff to appear at once, especially as I understand Casement told you he has no objection. However, I suppose this cannot be done.

Morel again makes a reference to 'your matter' which was to appear in *Regions Beyond*. Casement's request on behalf of the Foreign Office to Morel and Danielsen that they hold back prevented anything ever being published or written as far as we know.

Morel to Danielsen, 16 December 1903

I have written as follows to Mr. Guinness:

"Re photographs – I have almost completed my Congo book, which I hope will be published not very long after the official report comes out. I am anxious to send up the manuscript with the illustrations before Christmas.

Would it be possible for you to meet me to the extent of leaving me have advance copies of the photographs which you intend publishing in the Regions Beyond and which you intend lending me for the West African Mail.

I would of course pledge myself that these advance copies would not appear anywhere. I would be extremely obliged if you could see your way to do this ."

You of course quite understand that I do not want to publish the photographs. I merely want to send them up with my manuscript to my literary agent, who wants everything by Christmas.

Morel was persistent in his requests to use the photographs that Guinness now had, as is apparent from the following letter:

Morel to Guinness, 19 December 1903

Casement has made no arrangement with me about the photographs. Please let me have a copy of the one you purpose publishing in the Regions Beyond or send me the block.

What day in January will Regions Beyond come out? The West African Mail comes out every Friday.

I cannot make out from your letter whether you will be able to let me have any of the photographs for my book but if you can I should feel extremely obliged if you would have two copies of each developed and printed at my expense and let me have them at once as I am sending my completed manuscript to London with the illustrations this week.

It would appear from this that Guinness was still in doubt whether he would give the photographs to Morel or perhaps Casement's request had made Guinness more cautious. In this letter Morel is only asking for the photographs and not for testimony from Danielsen, because he was still waiting for Casement's report. Later in December Morel was still asking Guinness for the photographs he had:

Morel to Guinness, 31 December 1903
I should be obliged if you could let me have a copy of the photograph which is appearing in the Regions Beyond next month or lend me the block so I can have a couple of photographs made.

The photographs in print
E. D. Morel often published pictures without attributing his source for them. It is a problem for the whole period, not only for photographs from the CRA campaigns. *Regions Beyond* was illustrated, but the many photographs published of CBM stations were not attributed or properly catalogued

In early 1904 the *West African Mail* printed three photographs from the Congo. This corresponds with the letter Morel received from Guinness, dated 16 October 1903, saying that Guinness sent three of his photographs to Morel.[15] It was part of their agreement, that these photographs should not be published before the beginning of 1904.

In January and February 1904, *Regions Beyond* and the *West African Mail* printed the same photograph of a mutilated boy in their journals.[16] The caption in the West African Mail was 'through the kind favour of Dr. Grattan Guinness'. In the related article in *Regions Beyond* it is stated: 'Let the photograph we reproduce speak for itself – it is a message that demands a hearing. It shows a Congo child whose right hand has been shot off in the rubber palaver, in which his mother was killed.' This photograph was of Lokoto who lived in Mpelenge, three miles outside Bonginda. We know that Danielsen met him as he is mentioned in Casement's report.[17] This photograph was used

Let the photograph we reproduce speak for itself—it is a message that demands a hearing. It shews a Congo child whose right hand was shot off in the rubber palaver, in which his mother was killed. Such are the results of the desperate rubber *régime* which has blighted the Congo. "Rubber—rubber—at any cost—and quickly!" comes the cry of the monopolist, and the pressure is communicated from the Belgian clique, by means of intermediary officials, until, at last, by the gun of the native sentry it impinges in all its cruel severity upon the helpless inhabitant of the forest land, where grow the rubber-giving vines. And the blame lies not so much at the door of the savage, who in order to inspire the obedience of terror, and secure his toll of rubber, mutilates the defenceless, and raises a hell on earth wherever he is found—as at the door of those who maintain in active operation a system of forced labour so adjusted as inevitably to bring forth the crimson stain wherever it be applied.

It cannot be too clearly emphasised that *the system is fundamentally iniquitous and inhuman.* The axe of united European action must be laid

at the root of this tree, and those powers which have solemnly pledged themselves before Almighty GOD to watch over the welfare of Congo's millions, must carry into effect their self-imposed responsibility, by dealing with the terrible facts which have accumulated to such an extent as seriously to threaten with extinction the government which has nurtured and fostered this *régime* of terror.

We hope and pray that the answer of Europe to the voice of protest raised by the British Parliament, may be such as to warrant a hope that the crimson epoch of Congo mal-administration may speedily be terminated. In order in some measure to contribute towards this end, we are publishing in February an illustrated volume on the subject which will present the "Missionary Indictment of the Congo Administration," and we further propose to hold a series of important mass meetings throughout our land, to educate the people on this subject by means of lantern illustrations, and to support by resolution the action of the British Government.

H. GRATTAN GUINNESS, M.D.

The latter part of an article in Regions Beyond *January 1904 with the title* The Red Flower of Congo Civilisation. *The boy is Lokoto, almost certainly photographed by Danielsen.*

in the montage, described earlier (see p. 102). The second published photograph was of Mola Ekulite who was met in an ABMU station at Ikoko, and so on a part of Casement's trip for which Armstrong was not present.

On 26 February 1904, the *West African Mail* published the third atrocity photograph, which Morel likely had got from Guinness. The caption says that it was taken 'last autumn'. It is the photograph reproduced above (page 105) which, it was argued, is likely to show Danielsen; however, it is subtitled as a 'Swedish Missionary'. It is possible that if this is a misattribution, it was a result of Morel knowing Danielsen was Scandinavian, but mistaken in where he came from.

Morel was writing *King Leopold's Rule in Africa*, and included many photographs. Morel attributes three of them to Armstrong as CBM mission chief at Boginda.[18] One of these is the photograph of Lokata reproduced above. It was one of the three photographs which Guinness had given him in late 1903 from Danielsen. The book was being written at the same time as he was publishing these photographs in *West African Affairs*. The misattribution is therefore unlikely to have been due to carelessness. The pictures were published almost immediately after they were received. Nor is Morel unlikely to have misunderstood where the photographs came from as the above correspondence shows.

Morel may have erased Danielsen as a source as attempts had already been made to blacken his character.[19] The more substantial person of Armstrong, also connected to Casement, may have seemed like a better source. Danielsen was after all working class and a foreigner. Morel's lack of regard for him can be seen in the abrupt end to his correspondence as soon as the photographs have been handed over.

Morel did on occasion 'tidy' the evidence which he received from missionaries to make it fit better into his narratives. None of the changes he makes substantially affects the evidence presented. In one example Morel describes a photograph he has been sent in 1902.[20] He then describes the same photograph but claims to have been sent it in 1904.[21] The letter, copied into an appendix in *King Leopold's Rule*, reads like a composite of many letters sent from an ABMU missionary to Morel.[22] While no change has been made to the content Morel has reorganised and presented the evidence in the way most likely to persuade his reader.

This is the first and most important example of Danielsen being removed from his own history. Neither Morel nor Guinness mentions Danielsen in the early publication of his photographs. After 1904 Danielsen returned to the Faroes and no longer played an active part in the CRA campaign. As Danielsen's role was not properly recorded at this time he has been completely forgotten by history.

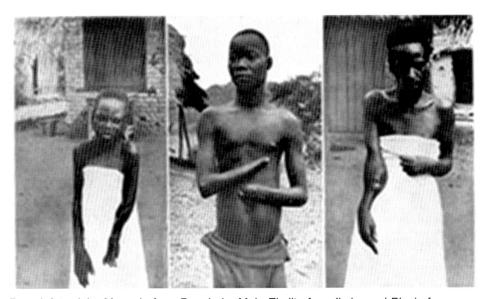

From left to right: Mongola from Bonginda, Mola Ekulite from Ikoko and Biasia from Bonginda. Casement wrote about Mongola and Biasia in his report: '(Local) people... brought with them a full grown man named Biasia, whose arm was shattered and greatly swollen through the discharge of a gun, and a small boy named Mongola, whose left hand was broken in two places from two separate gun shots'.

The photograph of Mola Ekulite was printed in Morel's West African Mail *19 February 1904.*

From the correspondence between Morel, Guinness, and Danielsen, it is probable that the photograph was brought to Britain by Danielsen. This block was also reproduced in King Leopold's Rule in Africa.

The photograph of Mola Ekulite was printed in Morel's West African Mail 19 February 1904 (see p.107).

PART TWO

MISSIONARY CAMPAIGNS IN THE FAROE ISLANDS

INTRODUCTION

1904 started a new chapter in Danielsen's life. He went to the Faroes on the 4th March and stayed until 4th May, during which time he held Congo and Biblical lantern lectures at least in two places, Tórshavn, the island capital on the east coast of Streymoy, and Viðareiði, the northernmost settlement on the Faroes on the island of Viðoy. Undoubtedly visits to there were no coincidence, as both places had two of the earliest and strongest Faroese Brethren assemblies (as the movement terms its congregations), then numbering no more than half-a-dozen. When the final decision was taken that he could not go back to the Congo, he and his new bride, Lina, took up residence in the Faroe Islands in July 1904. It must have occurred to Danielsen that the skills and characteristics he had developed had prepared him for missionary work there. He was a native speaker of the language of the people; he was a skilful sailor (essential for travel in the islands); he could accept great physical hardship; he had studied and preached the Bible; and he had learned to be a persuasive public speaker. These must have been factors in his decision. His health was another factor. Severely weakened by the Congo, a less fever-laden climate was advisable. He and Lina began their missionary work in different villages where in several of them they established new assemblies of the Brethren.[1]

The founder of the Brethren in the Faroe Islands was William Gibson Sloan, who was born 4 September 1838 in Dalry, in north Ayrshire in southwest Scotland. He had become a missionary and had been sent to Shetland by the Edinburgh Religious Tract and Book Society.[2] While in Shetland, Sloan had come into contact with Baptist churches and he had received believer's baptism, although he never became a Baptist. Later he had come in contact with the Brethren, and issues such as the 'breaking of bread' (as the Brethren term their communion services) had come up. In Lerwick in had 1864 he became one of the founder members of Shetland's first Brethren assembly. It was in this belief that in 1865 he had decided to become an evangelist to the Faroe Islands, which he had heard of from Shetland fishermen, who earned their living by fishing in their vicinity.[3] For many years, his work in Faroe had little effect, but eventually a few people had started gathering in the hall he had built (known in Faroe as 'Sloan's Hall') in Tórshavn in 1879. As the number of congregants was increasing, a new and bigger hall, Ebenezer, was built in 1906.

Faroes and neighbouring countries.

Danielsen was the first Faroese speaking full-time evangelist of the Brethren in the Faroe Islands. The move from an independent mission hall, in which he had been converted and the faith missionary principles of the CBM to the Brethren was an easy one to make. They shared the same revivalist evangelicalism, trust in divine providence, and lay ethos. Henry Grattan Guinness had been a member of the Brethren in Dublin, and Sloan himself had made the transition. Danielsen was described as rather harsh in his preaching, at least to begin with.[4] He and his wife settled in Tórshavn, and their home be-

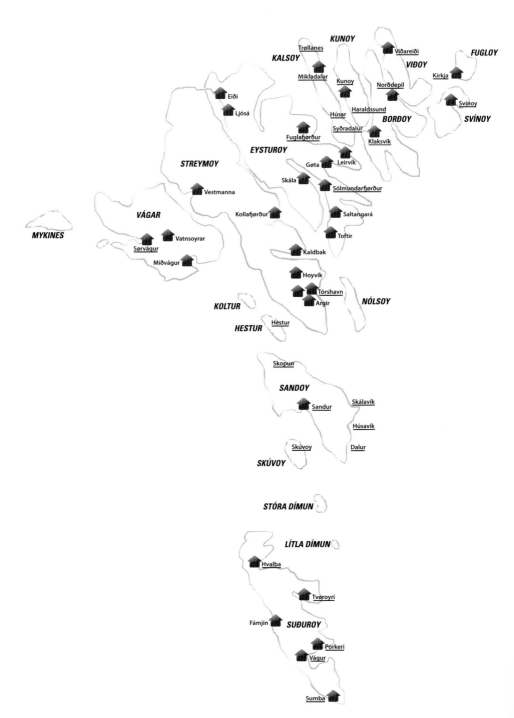

The maps shows the places where the Brethren
have and have had assemblies. The places Danielsen visited are underlined.

came a local meeting place for the young people in the assembly. These young people were fascinated by all the African things that were used to decorate the house.[5]

Danielsen's house in Tórshavn.

As we know from the Congo campaign, Danielsen was a very charismatic speaker. As has been noted above, while preaching in the Faroes he could bring the whole audience to sobbing. But he also had a sense of humour. A few anecdotes are still current in oral tradition. The reason he gave for not being eaten by the cannibals was that he was too thin! The other anecdote is that he encountered a very angry man at one of his meetings. He exclaimed, "Oh, I have seen much more furious men in Africa!" After that the man was silent. Danielsen was very puritanical. He once told Andrew William Sloan, the son of 'Old' Sloan (as W. G. Sloan was known in Faroe), that there was only one secular temptation he couldn't resist – a comic strip.

It has been demonstrated that he made a contribution to the Congo campaign. During his twelve years in the Faroe Islands, however, he also made a contribution to his own society. It was through his energetic work that the Brethren began to increase both in number and influence from 1904. After his death, Victor Danielsen (1894–1961), a cousin, and Andrew W. Sloan (1896–1973) continued his work and decisively advanced the Brethren cause in the Faroes which continued to grow, and eventually grew into the largest independent one in the islands, second only to the Danish Lutheran church, the established church. By the early twenty-first century, the Faroes had the largest percentage of Brethren in the world relative to the total population – some fifteen per cent.[6]

As had been in the Congo campaign, Danielsen was also a controversial person in Faroese society due to his clear opposition to the established Lutheran Church. In 1915 Danielsen, together with Arthur Brend, a British Brethren missionary, started a periodical, *Naade og Sandhed* [*Grace and Truth*]. The periodical of the Lutheran Church, *Færøsk Kirketidende* [*Faroese Church News*], advised people even not to read it. As it stated:

> You may say: It is harmless just to read, what they are writing, it would not make me a Brethren. But if people regularly are reading such stuff they step by step will be influenced by what they read, and those people will probably end up as Brethren. It is of course wise of the Brethren to publish a periodical, but if you on your side will be as wise as they are, don't let it come into your home.[7]

Unusually for a Faroese periodical of this time, *Naade og Sandhed* was illustrated which made it more appealing and accessible to readers. It is one more example of Danielsen's love of the visual.

While Danielsen had not always seemed to get along well with his all colleagues during his time in the Congo, there is no evidence to suggest this was replicated in his work in the Faroes. However, when Danielsen died, Arthur Brend wrote in *Naade og Sandhed*, that during his final illness, while staying in hospital in Copenhagen, he met love and care from everybody, but he was also a target for others for unchristian attacks on his work and character, which had a negative effect on his already broken health.[8] Although we do not know exactly what lies behind this statement, it probably alludes to the external forces that had opposed him in the Faroes.

D. J. Danielsen's Letters

There has been quite a lot written about the evangelistic work of Danielsen in the Faroes from 1905 until 1916.[9] It is for a great part based on some of his letters to *Echoes of Service*, the principal English-language Brethren missionary periodical, which is the best source for Danielsen's evangelistic work in the Faroe Islands. They start in 1905, the year after Danielsen's arrival to the Faroe Islands, and end in 1916, the year of his death. In the most cases he writes himself. Where he is mentioned in the third person, the writer is probably Arthur Brend (1880–1959). Brend was from London, and moved to the Faroes about the same time as Danielsen, and for many years he too worked as an evangelist with the Brethren.[10]

When reading the letters, it is useful to note that the Faroe Islands consist of eighteen individual islands – six large and twelve smaller. During this period there were no roads and very limited ferry connection between the islands. The most common methods of travelling in the islands were the use of open boats and walking. The Faroes are very mountainous, and their isolated position between the Norwegian Sea and the North Atlantic Ocean means the waters around them can be tempestuous and subject to sudden storms, especially in winter. Walking between settlements often meant strenuous trips over mountain paths, and travelling by boat was time-consuming and sometimes hazardous. Nevertheless Danielsen managed to visit the most of the islands, and many of them several times, and the arrival of steamboats as ferries, which we find him using in 1913, greatly eased inter-island travel.

These letters are part of Faroese Brethren history, but the descriptions of his travels are also a window into Faroese society at the beginning of the twentieth century. Most of all they are invaluable descriptions of Danielsen, and his methods. As he was writing for a missionary magazine, the letters concentrate on his missionary tours in more remote islands in the summer, although occasionally his activities close to home in Tórshavn receive a mention. A clear strategy emerges. His initial energies in his first few years were directed to the towns and villages where an assembly already existed due to the work of W. G. Sloan and his early associates. In the summer this activity was in the more distant northern islands, especially Viðoy, and the larger southern island of Suðuroy, where there already were assemblies. However, as these become more established, particularly from 1910 onwards, he extended his work into new places. The ultimate aim of Brethren evangelism was to gather the converts into autonomous self-governing assemblies. In these new places he would attempt to see the converts being gathered to form the nucleus of an assembly. As the Brethren have no ordained clergy, the members were responsible for all the congregational activities, and so it was necessary to teach and encourage them. Particularly of interest to him were places where a seed had already been planted due to someone being converted through one means or another. Some of these new assemblies came into existence within his lifetime, and others would be formed in the 1920s and 1930s. Clearly he saw himself as a pioneer, able to extend the Brethren into new places in the islands. Consequently more and more places are mentioned as the letters progress in time. He also used contemporary means for spreading his evangelical message, such as Lina accompanying his services with playing and singing, or using the magic lantern to illustrate the gospel message. The letters were accompanied with photographs. Danielsen knew the importance of those. It is not known if the photographs were taken by Danielsen himself, but it is possible that he continued to use a camera in the Faroes. It is in his spirit to reproduce them in connection with his letters. The letters are given in chronological order of writing, with comments and notes for explanation.

1905, Need and Work in Faroe

Viðareiði, the most northern village of the Faroes, is on the island of Viðoy. It was the first and main target of Danielsen. The reason may have been that his mother-in-law, Cathrine Niclasen, came from Viðareiði, but in addition it had earlier received the attention of W. G. Sloan, and one of the earliest and most influential assemblies in the Faroes had been formed there.[11] Later Danielsen's mother-in-law inherited a house which was used as meeting hall. In the letter below he describes his evangelistic meetings during 1905 in the village. Danielsen refers to his fellow workers as 'brother' (abbreviated here to 'Br.'), the custom from which the Brethren got their name. Hans Joensen (1854–1924), who accompanied him, was one of the first and leading brothers in Tórshavn. He was a businessman and had got his education and training in Leith, the port for Edinburgh. It was in Leith that he, too, later got his wife, Anette.

Faroe Isles.
Help from God in visiting one of the North Islands.
Thorshavn, Feb 15th. – I am just back from one of the Northern Islands, Viðoy. Br. Hans Joensen was with me; he is a good singer, and a little time away from business does him good; he is also very plain and simple in speaking the gospel. God help us all to be simple! We were nine days at that place, and finished with a prayer-meeting which the Spirit turned into a praise and testimony meeting.

At some of the gospel meetings both speaker and people broke into loud sobbing. The Spirit led me to speak of Calvary, and that can break our hard hearts. Pray that God will give us a deeper vision of Calvary, and lead us to see our unworthiness of all our Saviour's love. We have good reason to believe that many souls passed from death to life.

I have never experienced such a meeting before. The farmhouse where they were held was far too small; doors were taken off between rooms to accommodate the people, and still all could not get access. This makes much work for the wives of the farmers, who have to wash up after the people are gone, but they gladly lend their houses. The believers at Viðareiði are praying earnestly that God will enable them to get a larger place for assembling in. They are very poor and can only pray. God help them and strengthen their faith. They are mocked and scoffed at by the church party, but not many are against us; we have to go gently and prayerfully ahead. The Lord by His Spirit can open the priest's heart.

To get from island to island we need a small launch, which would not be too expensive to get nor to keep up; the need is great and the time is short. I have sold a quantity of Bibles and Testaments; they are cheap, so that the poorest can buy them; pray that they may be blessed greatly. The Brethren in Tórshavn are building a new Hall, and it will soon be ready to use.

D.J. Danielsen
(Formerly engineer of a Congo steamer.)[12]

Lina and Danielsen ready for a missionary expedition.

Danielsen found that the people had very little knowledge of the Bible. Usually people went to church on Sunday. The priest would only preach six times a year, and on the other Sundays a lecture would be read by a layman. But Danielsen found that there was a need for the people to read the Bible themselves. At that time the Bible was only in Danish, which everybody was able to read. It was not until 1949 that the Bible was printed in Faroese, translated by his cousin, Victor Danielsen.

Danielsen's next letter, which gives more details of the conditions in the Faroes and the origins of Brethren missionary work in the islands, was prefaced by a note from the editors of *Echoes of Service* drawing upon information supplied by Danielsen. Intriguingly, it was the only time after returning to the Faroe Islands he even mentioned his connection to the Congo.

Faroe Island

As it was said after Mr. Danielson's letter that he was "engineer of a Congo stea-mer," he writes to explain that he was not on one of the fifty trading charge vessels on the Congo, but that he had charges of steamers that carry the message of peace.

Mr. Danielson is a native of the Faroe Isles, but having as a boy been appren-ticed to engineering, he went to sea and travelled in many parts of the world. In Glasgow, in 1897,[13] he was converted to God, and had a great desire to study His Word and know His will. He much wished to go to the heathen and tell them of Jesus, and after being in South Africa for some time, he answered an advertise-ment for a Christian engineer for the Congo. Thus he went in 1901 as missionary engineer, and as soon as he had acquired a native language he preached the gospel. At the end of 1904 he had returned to his home, and as the climate had injured his health, he was led to give himself the gospel work in his native islands. He writes as follows:

Need and Work in Faroe Islands.

Thorshavn. – I speak the Faroese language and the people prefer it, although the Scriptures are printed in Danish. The native language is spoken in all homes and in schools, but all are compelled to learn Danish in schools, and nearly all lesson books are in the Danish language.

Ceremonies play a great part in the religion here, which is supposed to be ac-cording to the teaching of Martin Luther; but many are seeking after *God*, and in some country places we have precious times. In Viðareiði many are seeking, and a few profess to know Christ as their Saviour, but we have no meeting place. Farm kitchens are too small, and a hall here would greatly extend the work of the Lord. There are still many islands that have not heard the gospel in the old, simple way; but some of the seed that Br. Sloan has been sowing so faithfully for many years is beginning to grow. We have good reason to praise our heavenly Father for send-ing Br. Sloan to these Islands. He is getting aged and is not able to go about the country as before; but some motors boats have come, and some small steamboats are coming, we hear: so it will not be as difficult in the future, I hope.

Missionary work in these islands consists in great part of visiting from house to house, and I find that, being a native, I can sympathize with the people and speak to them more freely. In summer we have open-air meetings. The people in the county have nothing like there is in Tórshavn to draw their minds to the world and its glitter; everything is simple and plain, and those who are faithful cling to the precious Word of God above everything. God help us all to do the same!

D. J. Danielson[14]

In his next letter Danielsen describes the ordinary Lutheran upbringing he had received. The conventionality of such an upbringing was one point that counted against established religion for the Brethren, who favoured a personal faith, chosen by the individual. The southern island he refers to, where an assembly had been founded, is Suðuroy, the southernmost of the islands, where one had been formed in the village of Porkeri.[15]

Faroe Isles
Doctrines Learned in Childhood.
Thorshavn, August 22nd. – I have been to a few islands this summer, where I had good meetings, and sold a number of Scriptures. If people would only believe the Bible was really God's Word to them! Many never read it, while others think they confer a favour on God by doing so. Pray that the Lord may bless our testimony, and enable us to reach many in the far-off islands, where the darkness is great. From infancy the people are taught that they become children of God by being sprinkled as babes. I remember well when I was a little lad, my mother, while putting me to bed, would ask me a few questions, which I had to answer as follows: "Who made you?" "God the Father." "Who redeemed you?" "God the Son." "Who sanctified you" "God the Holy Spirit." "When did you become a child of God?" "In baptism." Nearly every mother follows the custom, and the same teaching is received at school and church.

Yet, praise be to God, where the light is shining all the darkness must go. Many of the old customs are now dying away. In one of the southern islands twelve are now breaking bread in a believer's house, and are happy in their new-found Saviour and Friend. Also in the north of Viðareiði a few worship God in spirit and in truth, as do a few more in some other islands. These must be visited often, for they have much to battle against. Kindly ask God's people to pray for the work in these parts of the vineyard.

D. J. Danielsen[16]

1906, Instructing New Converts

In his first letter of 1906 Danielsen shows that the established church is becoming concerned about the spreading of the new movement within the islands.

Instructing New Converts
Thorshavn, Faroe Isles, Feb 16th. – Since returning to Faroe after a short visit to Scotland, I have baptized eight believers, but now the [Lutheran] church party are holding lectures on infant sprinkling, and begging the people not to depart from

the old church customs. They say we are sinning against the Holy Spirit in baptising the people again, but still those that are anxious about their souls' salvation will come to our meetings, and a few have of late passed from death unto life, and are testifying that they have been in darkness, but have entered into light.

God willing, my wife and I are to-morrow going to Suðuroy, the most southern island. A young brother from Tórshavn has been there, and our heavenly Father has blessed his testimony, so that many have been saved, but now they need instruction in the Word. Pray for these new-born ones, for us and for the work. God has begun to work among the people, and many are feeling the burden of their sins.

D. J. Danielsen[17]

1907, Service and Need in Faroe Islands

In his first letter of 1907, Danielsen writes of a preaching tour to Vágar, the most westerly of the larger islands, and to Suðuroy. The letter gives considerable insight into his strategies for evangelising in Faroe.

Music was evidently important. Using an organ at services was very new at that time, and it was especially innovative to have a transportable one. Probably the one his wife played was a harmonium of the type that had been popularized in the late nineteenth century by the American singing evangelist, Ira D. Sankey, in the crusades of D. L. Moody. As the Faroese love singing, it gave Danielsen's services an extra attraction. At that time hymns were only available in Danish. He published a songbook *Evangelical Hymns for Use in Assembly and Home* with ninety hymns in Danish. This was the first hymn book of the Brethren in the Faroes. After his death, a booklet was also published with eleven English hymns that he had translated from English to Danish. It would be translations like these that he used at his services such as the ones on Vágar, and in other places as well.

Danielsen constantly looked for novel ways in which to reach his countrymen with his message. For his services on Vágar, Danielsen hired a dance hall. The Faroese ring dance was a part of the old Faroese culture, and the dancers would sing old ballads with up to 100 verses, sometimes more, while dancing. For that purpose dancing halls were built in the most villages which could also be hired for other purposes, such as evangelistic meetings. From the Congo campaign Danielsen knew how useful a magic lantern slide-show was. It is only in a few instances he mentions magic lanterns in the Faroes, but he evidently saw their potential, as the letter makes plain. He would have become familiar with their use in evangelistic contexts in the Glasgow mission halls, where 'gospel by limelight' meetings were held. They were widely used among the Brethren in Britain for missionary reports and children's evangelism. Danielsen evidently felt that it would be a way to communicate his message to those more resistant to attending one of his religious services.

Vágar was an island that had been visited by Sloan, and it is probably converts from his visits to Sørvágur to whom Danielsen refers.[18] The assembly in Porkeri was evidently growing, for it was building a hall. However, Sumbø on Suðuroy did not receive a Brethren assembly until the 1940s.[19]

'Mr. and Mrs. Danielsen have left for a missionary expedition.'

Faroe Isles
Part of a letter from D. J. Danielsen.

In the beginning of January I was led to go to Sørvágur,[20] a town with 500 inhabitants, in the island of Vágar. Two believers were residing there, but were not quite loosened from the old church ties, which abide very firm and rob believers of all liberty. My wife, who was with me, is a great help in the singing; sometimes we take the organ with us, as the people are very fond of good singing and are not able to sing our hymns. I hired a large dancing hall to preach in, and we got seats fitted up for about 100 people, but the first night over 150 people came, and the second over 250, and many had to stand outside, though all could hear.

This night the priest on the island came and spoke against us, telling the people they were made children of God by infant baptism, and they should hold on to the old ropes; but the people see these old ropes are not to be trusted. His speaking did not do much harm. I pointed the people to the Word of God and explained such passages as the priest used to defend infant sprinkling. The following night 150 people came. The baker of the town was converted, and rejoiced next day in his new-found Saviour, testifying to his friends and relatives. The people said he was mad, but praise God for all such. This man had been anxious for twelve years, and had tried in every way to get peace, but only got deeper in sin; now he has found peace and power to overcome.

A merchant in this town also accepted Christ as his personal Saviour. This man was quite careless about his soul, and told me one night after the meeting that his heart was as hard as a stone. A couple of days later he became so very anxious that he shut his shop and let the customers stand outside while he took me into his office to tell him the way of God. Before I left the town this merchant and his wife and servant were rejoicing and praising God for sending His only Son to die for him. I have heard since that he is testifying to his customers of his Saviour. Also the wife of one of the believers found peace with God, and these two are quite at liberty, so that now nine Christian in this place come together for prayer and the study of the Word of God. Surely we have reason to praise our Heavenly Father. These young believers have much persecution and need prayer. The priests of the church have been to this place to tell the people to hold fast; but it is not so easy for them to hold on when there is nothing to hold on to. Thank God, these souls, who have believed in the Lord Jesus, are sealed, and no one can separate them from the Saviour.

This place that I am now at is named Porkeri, a town in the island of Suðuroy. Last winter a few in this town came to the knowledge of the truth, and they have been growing in grace. There are twelve in number, and they are now building a small hall to assemble in; they are all working men and fishermen. I see a great difference in them since last winter, but we must visit them oftener with the Word, as some of them are not quite delivered from their old religion, and none of them are yet baptised. I have had three meetings here and spoken to two anxious ones. I visit the houses during the day and preach the Word in a big warehouse at night.

Sumbø is the most southern place in Faroe, and is only a little distance from here; the population is about 400. It will be difficult for me to get lodgings or a house to speak in, as the people there are yet in great darkness. I intend going over to the mountains to this place, and the Lord will open the door. We do not go in our own name, but in the name of Jesus, to whom is given all power in heaven and earth.

If I had a lantern with gospel pictures it would be very suitable for work up here, as in many places the people are afraid to come and hear us, because of the priest. I am sure many could be brought under the power of the Word through this means in spite of all the opposition. I ask the prayers of God's children that he will bless the Word spoken in all these different outlying islands where they seldom hear the gospel of the grace of God.

Because of their practice of believer's baptism, which involved baptising adults on a profession of faith by complete immersion in water, the Brethren were popularly called 'Baptists' in Faroe. The novelty of this practice made many Faroese wary of the new movement, as Danielsen's next letter of 1907 makes plain. The letter describes another trip to Suðuroy. Tvøroyri was the largest town on the island and was one of the principal Faroese fishing ports, with noticeable distinctions in social class. However, although some of its wealthier inhabitants were interested in hearing Danielsen, it would not have an assembly until 1921.[21] On the other hand, despite the initial opposition Danielsen and other Brethren experienced in Vágur, an assembly was formed there in 1909, only two years after Danielsen's visit.[22]

April 11th. – Since I last wrote I have been at Sumbø in the island of Suðuroy. The people would hardly lodge us at the beginning, but after the first meeting all was well and more come to hear the good news than we could find accommodation for. They bought many Bibles and gave us a warm invitation to come back soon, as they were longing to hear the Word again. No one had visited this place for twenty-one years, Br. Sloan having been the last.

I also visited Tvøroyri, the largest town in the island, and had a good meeting, larger than I ever had before. We got a hall, and many of the better-class people came to hear; some were seeking the way of life. Vágur, another town in this island, I could not obtain entrance to; they would neither give house nor Hall, being afraid I should make them Baptists. Now if I had requested a Hall to sing and show pictures in, I should have got it at once; it is in places places so prejudiced as this that the lantern would be useful.

There has been a good attendance at Tórshavn of late, but people are not so anxious to hear and accept the gospel as in other parts where it is seldom preached, though, praise the Lord, the work is going forward slowly but surely.

This has been a very severe winter, and since my return I have not been well. I may have to come south to consult a doctor, but we have a great Physician who is ever near "O Lord, increase our faith."

D. J. Danielsen[23]

W. G. Sloan's presence in the Faroes had attracted other Brethren missionaries, especially from among his fellow Scots, to work in the islands. Alexander Mitchell (1864–1939), who came from Glasgow, assisted Sloan from 1890 until 1899 and then again in 1905.[24] Duncan Campbell (*fl.*1890–1923), another Scot, worked with Sloan from 1903 until 1905.[25] However, the latter had to speak through an interpreter, and both men had left the islands for missionary work elsewhere, Mitchell for neighbouring Norway and Campbell for Denmark. In addition, Sloan was increasingly frail, being 69 by the time Danielsen wrote the next letter in 1907. The lack of evangelists to continue the work, and the difficulties imposed by the geography of the islands, obviously weighed on Danielsen. The letter is an appeal to a British audience for the needs of his homeland.

Service and Need in Faroe Islands.

Thorshavn, Dec, 15th. – For many years Br. Sloan has been faithfully sowing the good seed in these islands, and much blessing has followed his work, but at his present age he is not able to get about much in a part where travelling entails so many hardships. Messrs. Alex. Mitchell (now in Norway) and D. M. Campbell (now in Denmark) formerly laboured here; other Brethren also have stayed for a time, and the Lord has blessed the work done, the assembly in the capital numbering nearly forty, among whom are many bright lights. For two years and a half I have been assisting in the work, visiting from island to island as I have been able, but to many places where I have had invitations I have not been able to go on account of the expense. The way is open for the gospel in almost all the islands, and people are longing for us to come. There are, as you know, a few believers at various places, and they are praying for some-one to be sent to preach the Word. It is often pitiful to see, after a long absence, how Satan has robbed the young converts of their joy and simple faith. Owing to the difficulty of travelling up here, there is ample room for two or three evangelists.

D. J. Danielsen[26]

In his next letter Danielsen had been joined by another missionary, the Englishman Arthur Gook (1883–1959), who from 1905 had been a Brethren missionary to Iceland, and who would later become known as the translator into English of the classic Icelandic text, Hallgrímur Pétursson's Passion Hymns.[27] As the letter also makes plain, Danielsen now seems to have got a magic lantern which enabled him to get around the problem of a lack of suitable hymns by allowing him to project ones that were appropriate for his services. Brethren were strong believers in the imminence of Christ's second advent, and Danielsen shared this expectation, as the letter also shows.

In 1909 his visits to Sørvágur, on the island of Vágar, would produce fruit with the consolidation of the assembly there.[28]

Faroe Isles
The joy of Obedience
Thorshavn, Des. 13th. – Br. Gook from Iceland was with us for a fortnight, and we had a profitable time together and some extra meetings in Tórshavn. The Lord has enabled me to get a good lantern, with two gospel pictures, two hymns in Danish and many texts, and I have had some special meetings with it preaching the gospel. People came in crowds to see and hear, and many of these have since been to the ordinary gospel meetings.

Last Monday night I had the joy of baptising two dear brethren from Sørvágur, where a few were converted last winter. These are the first from that place to thus obey the Lord. The other day I had word by telephone from another brother, asking to be baptised. It is very touching to see this happiness of these dear ones afterwards; a deep, settled joy comes over them in knowing that they have done the will of God.

If the Lord tarry, I expect great things up here in coming days. Many doors are now open for the gospel. In numbers of places where no labourer has been for perhaps a dozen years I have now secured lodgings. The small country assemblies must also be often visited.

D. J. Danielsen[29]

1908, Dancing Hall Hire

Danielsen's first letter of 1908 shows how extensive his use of the dance halls was. As the letter makes plain, it was a neutral venue, and those who would not attend a building – either a house or a Brethren meeting hall – closely associated with the movement, would come and listen to him in a dance hall. The large town on Suðuroy where he hired one is probably Tvøroyri. However, even in places such as Hvalba on the same island, where an assembly had been formed in the previous century due to regular Brethren activity started under Sloan,[30] he also used one as a neutral meeting place. On this trip he visited two other islands where there were assemblies, planted by Sloan in the previous century. He again visited the island of Vágar, and that of Hestur, close to Tórshavn, where there had been a small assembly (possibly one of the earliest ones) since around the turn of the nineteenth century,[31] but he found little scope for the evangelism of outsiders, and so he took the opportunity to do some Bible teaching with its members.

Thorshavn, May 27th. – On March 16th I left for Suðuroy, the most southern island, and visited every town in the northern half of it. God willing, I hope to take the other half later on. In three of the towns I had a week's meetings, and in the largest I had the dancing-hall crowded every evening. In another town, Hvalba, there is a little assembly, and I found the believers healthy in soul and body, but others would not come to their houses for meetings, so here also I hired the dancing-hall. It was crowded for two nights, but the owners would not let me have it longer, so we managed to secure the loan of a boat-house. It was a draughty place and not very suitable, so but few came, but we had a blessed time, and the Lord worked with us. At the third place I got the dancing-hall more readily, and had a good attendances, a few enquiring the way of salvation. Since my return I have sent over thirty Bibles and Testaments to these places, besides a few sold while there, and at this time, in Faroe, Bibles are not bought to lie on the shelf. They are procured for many reasons – some to search in with a view to proving us wrong in our teachings, others to compare the old faith, as the people call it, with what we say, but the most to search in them for a Saviour, and blessed be God, those who seek Him there will find him.

On April 13th I baptised a sister from Vágar, who was in the service of a baker at Tórshavn, she was immediately dismissed, but another door was opened for her, and she is rejoicing. A brother from the same island has been baptised since.

On April 16th I left for the island of Hestur, where a few believers have resided for many years, and others have been added of late. The people did not attend the gospel meetings well, but the Christians were thirsting for the Word.

D. J. Danielsen[32]

1909, Service of Visiting

Occasionally *Echoes of Service* printed a short synopsis of Danielsen's letters rather than printing them in full, as is the case here. It describes two of his preaching tours, firstly to the southern island of Suðuroy, and then to the northern isles (the latter tour is described first in the letter). Initially, he is again in Viðareiði on Viðoy, then on Svínoy, one of the smaller northern islands with a population of around 200, and finally to the similarly-sized island of Fugloy. In the latter place there were two villages, Kirkja and Hattarvík. The letter also shows that there was a growing tolerance from the government to the presence of the Brethren, and changes in the law to accommodate them greatly eased their position in Faroese society. Brethren tolerance can also be seen, for the leading individual in the Porkeri assembly and his wife had evidently not submitted to the rite of believer's baptism before he had became a leader.

Faroe Isles. – Mr. Danielsen continues his service of visiting the different islands for meetings, and a friend has kindly sent us a copy of a letter lately received from him. The little group of believers at Viðareiði had been somewhat hampered by the lack of a meeting-place but this has now been provided, and at the opening meeting it was full to the door and much interest was manifested, some asking the way of life. At Svínoy a large farm-house kitchen was so full that the speakers could hardly get in, and many bibles were ordered. At Kirkja, on the most northern island, a young couple were found rejoicing in the Lord who were converted at the hall at Tórshavn a year ago, when visiting that place in order to see the King of Denmark [who was on visit]. They have now a little child, whom their neighbours call a little heathen, as he was not been "christened." Here also there were good meetings.

During the earlier tour Mr. Danielsen baptised the leading brother of the little assembly of Porkeri, and also his wife. The latter was so weak she had to be led to the water, but she said afterward, "Now I am happy; I should not have liked to meet the Lord Jesus face to face unbaptised, for I have seen it so long and not obeyed. Now I can die in peace whenever the Lord wills it so." At one other place

The new Ebenezer, built in 1905, the assembly hall of the Christian Brethren. To identify the building, the name had been written on the photograph when it was originally reproduced.

a believer's child had died, and a little service was held in the cemetery, a new law permitting this, whereas formerly it had to be outside, and people said that our brethren buried their dead "like dogs." The change is an answer to prayer.[33]

1910, A Change from Former Days

By 1910 Danielsen was able to report the progress the Brethren were making, with several small assemblies forming a chain across the islands that offered friendly faces to the itinerant evangelist. However, as his letter in this year also shows, the reception he received was still mixed. Eysturoy, with which the letter begins, is one of the two large central islands in the Faroese archipelago.

Faroe Isles
A Change from Former Days

Thorshavn, June 25th. – Since returning from Scotland I have been to the island of Eysturoy, where I visited with the gospel all the homes in three villages. The reception varies: in a few houses one meets faces hard as marble and looking as though they would freeze one through, but a kind word often melts the hard look, so that we are able to leave a gospel leaflet, and often the reception is better next time. In other homes we are asked to sit down, and in some we are made welcome and the people lay down their work and listen attentively. Often people from neighbouring houses come to hear, and we have an earnest kitchen meeting.

Some time ago I returned from the town of Sørvágur, where the believers were glad to see me, and we had a blessed time of fellowship. I had a few meetings and visited forty houses, being on the whole well received. A few days before my arrival a sister was baptised and then left for summer work in Iceland. This young woman was converted on our last visit, just before we went to Scotland.

In a few days I hope to visit the northern islands, taking my dear wife to assist in the work. There is a small hall in Viðareiði, as you know, but it is too small for gospel meetings, and many have to stand outside, especially in the winter. This was a dwelling-house altered, as ground on which to build a new hall was refused, but now the Lord has graciously opened the way in a wonderful manner, for I have received permission from the government to build a hall on a piece of ground in the middle of the town, a most suitable place, a few believers reside at Viðareiði, none of whom have yet been baptised, but two families have broken from the old customs and desire to follow the Lord according to His Word only. The head of one of these has named a sum that we and his wife have agreed to give toward the hall. The people there are usually poor, but others have offered to assist, and the proceeds of the sale of our old hall will help. This will be the fourth gospel hall built in Faroe within five years, and soon the brethren on a southern island hope to put up another. A few years ago you might go through some of these towns without finding any Christian fellowship, and perhaps not even a friendly look or smile (if on the Master's errand), but to-day what a change! You get a hearty welcome and enjoy Christian love, and may meet in a neat little hall with a few men and women whose faces are lit up with happiness and holy joy. We shall value prayer for the Lord's work in these lonely islands.

D.J Danielsen[34]

1911, Retrospect

In his letters of 1911 Danielsen was able to report the progress of the Brethren throughout the islands, when he visited places that had been mentioned in earlier letters. The summer made travel by sea easier, and he was able to travel widely throughout the islands, from north to south, during the summer season.

> *Tórshavn, Faroe, Jan. 30*[th]. – I send a few lines to cheer God's people who have for years been praying for His work in these lonely islands. In the middle of December my wife and I sailed to the northern island, Viðoy. The village Viðareiði has a population of 300, and as the new gospel hall was just ready for use, we began special meetings after some nights of prayer. I was enabled to hold thirty gospel meetings, besides others for God's people, and in some homes we are asked to have meetings after a friendly cup of tea. The hall was sometimes crowded, and never before had I seen such a blessed time there. One night five stood up, one after the other, and testified of a new-found Saviour. During the meetings nine souls confessed Christ openly. A good many Bibles were sold, and many are searching the Scriptures.[35]

Danielsen was finding increasing attention for his preaching in the northern islands of Fugloy and Svínoy, islands which would eventually have assemblies on them. The greater reception his message was receiving could be seen in Vágur on Suðuroy, where he found he had been shut out as recently as his letter of 11 April 1907.

In this next letter he notes that two people have travelled for believer's baptism from Viðareiði to Tórshavn where Sloan's Hall had an indoor tank for the purpose. A number of other baptisms in Faroe would be performed in the sea.

Faroe Isles.

Retrospect of the Summer's Work

Thorshavn, Sept. 11th. – Now that the summer will soon close, we are very thankful to our God for His preserving care and His great goodness in opening the way for us to reach a good many places with the gospel. In summertime indoor meetings are not as a rule well attended, but those in the open air are, and the people will stand listening for any length of time. This gives us an opportunity to reach many who will never come to an indoor meetings. Visiting the people in their homes has proved a great blessing, as many who will not come to a meeting are glad to have a quiet talk at their own firesides.

In the summer we also endeavour to visit believers in isolated places, and sweet is the fellowship enjoyed on such occasion. During May and the first half of June I visited the northern islands of Fugloy, Svínoy and Viðoy, and had encouraging gospel meetings in every village on them. On the next island, Borðoy, I visited two villages, in the larger of which (Depli) I managed to hire the dancing-hall, and had two gospel meetings; not many attended, but in visiting I found the people very friendly. On such visits the people often ask for copies of the Word of God, which I have joy in supplying. At Viðareiði I found the believers happy in Christ, and progressing in the ways of God. Since my last letter two more from that place have been baptised at Tórshavn, one of them being a man seventy-eight years old of age.

After spending time in Tórshavn, assisting in the work in this needy town, I proceeded to the southern island, Suðuroy, where I visited several of villages. At Hvalba I baptized a young sister, the daughter of a believer. Many people assembled to witness it, so we had an earnest gospel meeting. On my way back to Tórshavn I made a stay in the town of Vágur, which has about eight hundred inhabitants. Here we had, I think the largest open-air meeting I have seen in Faroe. The people listened earnestly to the Word, and afterwards a few shook hands with us and thanked us for coming. Some of the friends from Porkeri were present and testified of the Lord's saving power, for the place is only two miles from there. Five years ago could not get lodgings at Vágur. Now we are welcome and know of five believers there. Join with us in prayer that the seed sown may be blessed to many souls.

To-morrow my wife and I hope to leave for the western island of Vágar for some gospel meetings at the town of Sørvágur.

D. J. Danielsen[36]

1912, Two Kinds of Fishing

In his first letter of 1912 Danielsen again describes his tour of the islands. It starts on the southernmost island, Suðuroy, where he again visits Tvøroyri.[37] Viðareiði, and its assembly on the northern island of Viðoy, formed a regular part of his itinerary by now. He was also preparing the way for assemblies that would come into existence in the 1920s. One place which he visits on this trip, and which would eventually become a significant Brethren centre, was Fuglafjørður, on the central island of Eysturoy. It would produce a steady stream of converts. Similarly, also on Eysturoy, at Søldarfjørður, an assembly would soon come into existence. Danielsen's maternal uncle there was his namesake, Daniel J. Danielsen, the local shriff and the father of his cousin, Victor, who was soon to be one of the most significant accessions to the new movement.[38]

Faroe Isles. – Mr. Danielsen writes of visits of some the islands. Truly encouraging meetings were held on Suðuroy. Especially at Tvøroyri, and signs of blessing were seen. The believers at Viðareiði, on Viðoy, asked for a visit before the fishermen went to sea; they are growing in grace and knowledge, and a sister was baptised. Four gospel meetings were held in the dancing-hall at Fuglafjørður, on Eysturoy, but not many attended, as the people had been displeased by the baptism of two young women from that place, who were in service at Sørvágur. These sisters have now returned home, and will be much persecuted. It was a joy to meet a woman at Fuglafjørður who had been converted while on a visit to Tórshavn, where she had attended one meeting. Her open confession of salvation through faith in Christ had much annoyed her family, who, like most Faroese, put infant sprinkling in the place of faith. Much interest was manifested at Søldarfjørður, on the same island, where an uncle of Mr. Danielsen opens his house for meetings; he is a believer.[39]

The livelihood of the people was mainly fishing, both coastal fishing, using small open boats, and increasingly deep-sea fishing around Iceland with smacks. The smacks were old sail-ships without any facilities, such as an engine or radio. They usually sailed for Iceland in March, coming back in May, again going for Iceland in June and coming back in September. The crew was typically fifteen to twenty men. Unfortunately quite a number of those smacks would not return and just disappeared, and that caused tragedies in many homes and villages. The same happened to the smaller boats. Many, many fishermen lost their lives at sea. In 1920 alone, sixty fishermen drowned out of a population of 20,000.

The Brethren movement in the Faroes grew alongside the development of commercial deep-sea fishing. One the leading first generation of Faroese Brethren, Napoleon Andreasen (1868–1912), familiarly known as Poli i Dali, had been honoured by the Danish king in 1907 for his pioneering work in the new fishing industry in Faroe. When not at sea, he had preached and held missions in various places. His death at sea, described in the first letter here, when he was only 44 years old was a great loss to the Brethren movement in the islands.[40] As the boats did not fish on Sundays, services were held for the crew. Evangelicalism has often appealed to those in dangerous occupations, and fishing communities have had pride of place among them. Such was the success in the Faroes of Brethren evangelising their fellow crew members while at sea that fishing boats became known as 'Cathedrals at Sea'.[41]

The next several letters demonstrate some of the dangers fishing presented, but also the opportunities for Brethren evangelism.

Danielsen's Bible, the only remaining memento of him in the Faroes.

Faroe Isles

Mr. Brend (a British Missionary) writes of the great sorrow that has fallen upon the brethren in these islands through the loss at sea of one of their numbers, Napoleon Andreasen, whose name has occasionally been mention in letters, and the crew of his fishing smack. The mate was also a believer in fellowship. The boat was expected home by Whitsuntime, but some weeks later nothing had been heard of it. Our brother Andreasen was much honoured and respected in the islands, having been made a Knight of the Dannebrog by the late King Frederick,[42] on account of a fishing expedition to Greenland and other services. He leaves a widow and a large family, and the mate also leaves a widow and child.[43]

Two Kinds of Fishing – D. J. Danielsen

Thorshavn, June 5th. – The fishing season is so far promising, but it is a dangerous occupation, and even now some are longing anxiously for dear ones who went to Iceland to the early fishing and have not yet returned. Many of the brethren go fishing, and the Lord has of late years granted much blessing among the fishermen. In many of these smacks the gospel is proclaimed to the men by life and word. As a rule the Faroese fisher does not cast a line overboard on Sunday, so this gives good opportunities for the Christians on the boats. A dear brother from the north islands, who is a skipper on one of these vessels, came back last season with good catch of fish and with two of his men who had professed conversion. Surely our brother had been fishing well! May our good God endue these brethren with all needed strength and grace for this double fishing!

On our last journey to the southern part of the island Suðuroy, we were greatly encouraged to see how wonderfully God has opened a door for the gospel which had practically been closed. In the town of Vágur, with about 800 inhabitants, we have had open-air meetings, but there has been difficulty in hiring a hall. Now, when even the dancing hall was not available, the way was opened. The merchants and others in the town have a club, with well-furnished halls and rooms, and this place they very kindly placed at our disposal at a very moderate charge. On some nights the hall was full, and much interest was manifested. Some of the members of the club came to the meetings, and we trust that a lasting work was accomplished.

We found Christians at Porkeri, east of Vágur, bearing a bright testimony for the Lord. We had a cheering time with them and the gospel meetings were well attended.[44]

1913, "Fishers of Men"

Danielsen's first letter of 1913 is again an account of his summer island tour. The assemblies at Porkeri and Vágur, on Suðuroy in the south, and Viðareiði in the north again received his attention. He also visited some of the smaller islands: Sandoy, where an early assembly had been planted by Sloan,[45] and Skúvoy, both to the north of Suðuroy; and the northern islands of Kunoy and Kalsoy, where assemblies would later be formed. Fuglafjørður, on Eysturoy, was emerging as an important centre for the Brethren, and he held cottage and open-air meetings with the small group of Brethren there. In the north he also visited Klaksvík, on Borðoy, which would eventually develop into the second-largest town in the Faroes. The Brethren would soon build a hall there, and it grew into one of the largest Brethren centres in the islands. The letter also shows how Danielsen contextualised his message in the Faroes by using the imagery of sea storms and fishing to make a simple religious point.

Faroe Isles
Review of the Summer's Work

Thorshavn, Oct. 17th. – As I write, the storm is shaking our wooden hut, and the sea, which only a little ago was like a sheet of glass, is angrily rolling against the rocks. One feels it is good to be in shelter, and our thoughts centre on the blessed shelter that is ours in Christ.

The fishing season is over, and has been a fairly favourable one. The two brethren mentioned in my last letter, are home, and during the season four on one ship have professed conversion, while on the other nine, precious souls are rejoicing in salvation. They seem not to be able to keep quiet, but must tell others of their new-found Saviour. This is good fishing indeed! Praise God with us. We ever keep before the Christians that they are saved to become fishers of men.

The summer gospel work has been very encouraging. We spend June here and in the district, and the open-air meetings were large. In July we visited the villages Vágur and Porkeri on the southern island, distributing tracts and holding some meetings, but the people were very busy out-of-door. The end of the month we spend at Viðareiði in the north, having hearty meetings with the believers, and four were baptised (a married couple, and the wives of two brethren in the assembly) In August I was permitted to make a stay in the island of Sandoy to the south-west, and five villages there were visited with the gospel. In two I got the dancing-hall for meetings, and had good attendances. Much interest was manifested, and some Bibles were desired. These I always carry with me. Since my return I have had cheering letters from a few persons there. The little island of Skúvoy, with a small village, was also visited, and the people asked us to call again soon.

In September I passed another week at Viðareiði, and thence went by motor-boats to the island of Kunoy and Kalsoy, to the north-west, where I had good meetings in farm-kitchens. From there I proceeded via Klaksvík to the village of Fuglafjørður on Eysturoy, where I had open-air meetings for eight evenings, besides homely gatherings with a few believers residing there. An aged woman who has been much prayed for (her sons being in fellowship) found peace with God and openly confessed Christ. She had been formerly a great opponent of the truth. The clergyman was sent for and spoke to her, but she pleaded that she had been blind and in darkness and now she saw. There was not much to be said, for it is vain to deny life; it speaks for itself. Those newly converted have good deal of persecution to endure. Pray that they may be kept steadfast and be guided by the Word of God alone.

D. J. Danielsen[46]

The developing strength of the movement can be seen in the chain of places Danielsen links on this trip – Viðareiði, Sørvágur, Klaksvík, Fuglafjørður, Søldarfjørður, and Tórshavn – that were to develop into significant centres for the Brethren in Faroe. The contrasts in the seasons of the year are very marked in Faroe, and due to the rhythms of fishing and farming, the people are very aware of the changes. The letter starts with simple biblical lessons drawn from nature that gives us an idea of the type of illustration Danielsen would use in preaching. Brethren scepticism about the spiritual value of the Christian year can be seen from the placing of inverted commas round Easter.[47]

Faroe Isles.
"Fishers of Men"
Thorshavn, May 7th. – It is a pleasant to see the fields changing their frosty mantle for their soft green summer one. Trees and flowers are rare indeed here, but if we cannot "consider the lilies" we may consider the grass and praise God for His never-failing faithfulness. The fishing season is not very promising as yet, that they may look to Him, who is able to fill their nets and is longing to save their souls.

In the latter half of February we made a stay at Viðareiði, a village of three hundred people with a healthy assembly of about twenty-five. We had a meeting every night for ten days, and rejoice in seeing fruits of the gospel. Three believers were baptised.

In the first part of March we had some gospel-meeting at Sørvágur, whence we proceeded by steamer to Klaksvík, the largest town in the northern islands. We had gospel meetings at "Easter" in the hall, which we hired. They were well attended, and much interest was manifested. Our hymns were sung and whistled in the streets and homes. I doubt not that the gospel message was pondered in many hearts, and marks were left for eternity. One night while we were there two fishing-smacks from Viðareiði were in, and the skippers, who were in fellowship, brought their crews to the meeting. Eleven testimonies were given that night to the saving and keeping power of our Lord and Saviour. Although the skippers had caught but little fish, they had done some successful fishing. Four of the crew had been saved on board one ship and two on board the other, since they went to sea this season. It was touching to hear their earnest testimonies, and many were moved to tears when these young sailors told how they had been taking the gospel bait and were landed safe on the Rock, and of the joy and peace that were theirs now. Yes, many saw and understood that there is power in the blood.

Afterwards we made a few days' stay at Fuglafjørður on the eastern island, where two sisters and the brother reside, the latter being a newly converted drunkard. Pray for these, for they have not a little persecution to endure. We had a large open-air meeting, and visited some houses. *En route* to Tórshavn we made a little stay at Søldarfjørður.

Dear Mr. Sloan is in about usual health, and I am glad to say, and frequently takes part in the meeting. We have splendid open-air gathering in Tórshavn just now.

D. J. Danielsen[48]

1914, Mr. Sloan's Burial

In the spring of 1913 Sloan had set on a final tour of Scotland during which he had given reports of the progress of the Brethren in the Faroes. He had returned to the islands in September exhausted, and his health would not fully recover from the trip. The outbreak of war in August 1914, and the knowledge that many young men would die, worried him greatly. He spoke for the last time at the assembly in Tórshavn on Wednesday 2 September, When he awoke on the Friday he felt ill, and he returned to bed. That evening, after praying with his family, he died.[49] Danielsen was in Porkeri on Suðuroy when he received the news, and he returned to Tórshavn to participate in the funeral service. His letter to *Echoes of Service* that year describes the funeral and pays tribute to Sloan.

Faroe Isles
Mr. Sloan's Burial
***Thorshavn, Sept. 14*[th]**. – It was at Porkeri, just before the Lord's-day morning meetings, that I learned of our beloved brother Mr. Sloan's home-call; and on Monday I returned to Tórshavn by motor-boat, accompanied by six brethren representing the two small assemblies in the island of Suðuroy. Tuesday, the day of the burial, arose beautiful and calm, and friends came from the assemblies at Viðareiði on the north and Sørvágur on the west. The coffin had been placed in the hall the previous day, and many of the townspeople desired to see our brother's peaceful remains. The hall was filled before the service began, and many had to stand outside. It was a solemn hour, and all felt the loss of a true friend. Some of Mr. Sloan's favourite hymns were sung, and a local brother, Mr. Brend and I gave a short gospel address, after which eight of the elder brethren carried the coffin to the cemetery. It was the largest funeral procession ever seen at Torshavn. The state church dean and two elder clergymen, people high and low, religious and irreligious, were among those who did honour to the memory of our departed brother, joining the procession to the grave, where Mr. Brend and I spoke briefly to the great crowd who respectfully stood around.

Our brother is at home with the Lord after many years of faithful service on these lonely islands. The first years were especially full of hardships and trials, and Mr. Sloan had often to experience want and persecution. The church in Faroe has lost a father, a shepherd and a most earnest gospel worker. In times of difficulty our brothers always had wise counsel to give, and in love everything was decided by "Thus saith the Lord." In times of rejoining he was the happiest among us, and what always gave him the greatest joy was to hear of souls being won for the Master. When one came from outlying places and told our brother of souls having professed conversion and saints being encouraged, he would motion with the hand, and say: "Let us thank God together for His goodness, and ask for still greater things." Still his work and life is speaking, and his memory will never be forgotten, while his reward is sure.

D.J. Danielsen[50]

The masthead of Naade og Sandhed with Tórshavn in the background.

1915, A Season of Blessing

In January 1915 Danielsen and Arthur Brend began their magazine *Naade og Sandhed*. A note in *Echoes of Service* describes its commencement:

Mr. and Mrs. Danielsen have been visiting out-lying places. At Sørvágur some of the children of the believers were brought to Christ. Mr. Brend and Mr. Danielsen have after earnest prayer commenced a monthly gospel paper called Naade og Sandhed (Grace and Truth), and a good number have subscribed for it. Such a periodical was much needed in Faroe. Mr. Danielsen asks us to thank the friend who supplies him with Echoes.[51]

A later note showed that *Naade og Sandhed* had been an immediate success: 'Messr. Brend and Danielsen have well over 600 subscribers to their periodical, and fifty or more persons receive it each month freely, while several hundred copies are given away as tracts.'[52]

Although Denmark and its territory of the Faroes were neutral in World War I, hostilities brought fresh hardships to the people. Deep-sea fishing also continued to be dangerous, and Danielsen's letter in 1915 both describes its effects and an additional hazard. The hunting of pilot whales was for centuries one of the most important food supplies in the Faroes. The incident mentioned in this letter, which took place in Sandvík, the village north of Hvalba, was the most serious one in the islands that happened in whale catching. The Scottish Brethren missionary in Singapore, Alexander Grant (1832–1914), had recently died, and a bequest made in his memory allowed Danielsen to distribute free Bibles among the bereaved. The itinerary Danielsen follows over the winter months of 1914–15 was by now a familiar one.

A Season of Blessing. D.J. Danielsen
Thorshavn, Feb 19th. – Shipping to and from these islands has been greatly interrupted during the war, and the consequences have been very severe for the inhabitants, for the price of everything is very high. Still we are confident that our all-wise God and loving Father is over-ruling all for good. Many have through trouble and reverse of circumstances been drawn to the Saviour's feet, and our gospel efforts have been crowned with much blessing.

In December we paid a visit to the Northern Islands, where about a year ago so many widows and orphans were left, the bread-winners being lost at sea while fishing. Through the kindness of some friend in London, in memory of Mr. Alexander Grant, I have been enabled to present each widow with a Bible, and these were gratefully received. We were much encouraged in the north by seeing many of God's people going on in holiness of life, and the Lord adding to the church "such as received salvation" (Danish Version).

In January I had a series of meetings at Sorvágur on the island of Vágar. Much interest was manifest, and fruit for eternity was seen. One night, after a meeting, four children of Christians were weeping under the burden of sin, and next day they professed to have trusted Christ as their Saviour.

We have just returned from the southern island, Suðuroy, and in Vágur, a town of eight hundred inhabitants, where some Christians reside, we hired a public hall and had seventeen gospel meetings. We had the joy of seeing and hearing of sinners finding peace with God. On some nights testimonies were given to the saving and keeping power of the Lord Jesus, and we rejoiced to see fruit of Br. Brand's last visit to this place. The talk of the town had been concerning the meetings and those who profess Christ, and Satan has all his instruments at work to hinder the people from coming to the meetings, so that many anxious and sin-burdened ones have been prevented from coming to hear the life-giving Word. Pray for such. In the house where we lodged there were seven children, and one boy of eight and a half was the heart-break of his Christian parents. After the meeting one night his mother urged him to accept Christ. Early next morning his father saw him kneeling at the bed side, and at morning worship, after breakfast, the boy joined for first time in prayer, thanking God for giving His Son to die for him.

Several times this winter my health has been failing, there apparently being something wrong with my heart, but it is now somewhat better. Pray that it may keep up, and that all needed grace may be given. My wife has been enabled to be with me on all my journeys this winter, assisting in the work.

As I write, I have received a letter from the next place we intend to visit (Hvalba on the island of Suðuroy) saying that, while whale-catching, two of the boats turned over in the breakers near the town and fourteen of the men lost their lives. In a few days we expect to be among the bereaved ones.

Br. Brend is at present in the island of Kalsoy.

D. J. Danielsen[53]

Sloan had from his early years in Faroe visited villages on Sandoy, an island between Tórshavn and Suðuroy. An assembly had been established on the east of the island at Skálavík which would later move to Sandur.[54] Danielsen was therefore following an established evangelistic trail when he visited the island villages. Lina Danielsen's singing again proved an attraction, and so too did the dental work that Arthur Brend, an exceptionally popular man, combined with his missionary service. Again the letter, with its references to Jesus as a sacrificial lamb and his longing to save, gives some idea of the content of Danielsen's preaching. The biblical imagery would be readily understood by the Faroese. Sheep were the commonest domestic animal on Faroe, and their annual slaughter was an established part of the farming year.

Mr. Danielsen: My wife and I have just come back from a journey to the south and western islands. In Suðuroy we made a stay at Tvøroyri, where we distributed gospel literature, visited houses and found isolated believers going on in the way of God. At the town of Hvalba and Vágur we had encouraging times and had meetings as opportunity afforded. We next went to Sandoy, which has not been much visited with the gospel. The people were very friendly and we were asked to go to some small villages, but the way was not open. We stayed at three towns on the island – Skálavík, where a Christian family lives, Sand, the largest place on the island and Skopun. We were very heartily received by the people. They were delighted with my wife's singing, and some came from distant places for dental advice (of Brend) and help. Houses were visited and we were asked to call to see sick people, so many opportunities were afforded to tell of the Lamb of God, a longing Saviour, and we had gospel meetings when we had opportunity. Mrs. Sloan's youngest son (Andrew William) is helping in the assembly at Thorshavn.[55]

1916, Fallen Asleep

The Brethren were not the only new religious movement in the Faroes in this period. Seventh Day Adventists (so-called because they worship on Saturday instead of Sunday) were also active, and their other fundamental differences from his views troubled Danielsen. This was the reason for his views on the Adventists in his letter of 1916. Although the Brethren proved to be the most successful and enduring among the new groups, a few Adventists are still present in the Faroes.

More heartening was the news from Søldarfjørður on Eysturoy. The local schoolmaster, Victor Danielsen, who also happened to be D. J. Danielsen's cousin, had experienced an evangelical conversion. After a few months he had resigned his post, as he could not agree with all the religious teaching of the Danish state schools. He had also begun to write for the periodical *Naade og Sandhed*, and it would be largely through his writing that he would become the principal figure in the coming generation of Brethren. He would translate the Bible into idiomatic Faroese, and write and translate numerous hymns.[56] In the early twentieth

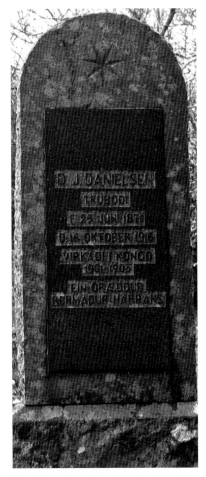

Danielsen's gravestone in the old cemetery in Tórshavn.

century there was a national movement in Faroe with as one of its aims, to preserve and maintain the Faroese language. The Brethren were leaders in the movement and started in the 1920s to use Faroese hymns. Victor Danielsen later wrote and translated around 900 hymns himself. Sadly, the letter in which D. J. Danielsen describes the emergence of the outstanding leader in the next generation of Faroese Brethren was to be his last.

Families converted

Thorshavn Jan, 27th. – During the past year we have been enabled to proclaim the gospel in various outlying islands and villages. Sin-burdened souls have found peace with God the cross, and believers have been encouraged to follow the Saviour in obedience and holiness of life, but the enemy of souls is busier than ever in sowing his evil seed of discord here and there, and in holding out to the hungry that which is not bread. The Seventh-day Adventists are working very hard to spread their erroneous literature among the people, and other sects seem to be springing up. We endeavour to circulate God's Holy Word, which is the only antidote against all error and reveals the true way.

At Søldarfjørður, a village of Eysturoy, God has been blessing His Word to many souls – a farmer, his wife and six children, another farmer, his wife and four children of the greatest opponent in the place. Victor Danielsen, the young school-master in this village, was lately converted to God. He resigned his place in the school, as he had to teach error to the children, and began to tell people, by pen as well as by personal testimony, of his Saviour. It pleased God to use him, and many more were led to Christ. His father, a retired district judge, has for many years been a true Christian, and was a great friend of our departed brother Sloan, who was often there in former years, telling out the good news, and in later years I have often had meeting there. Last December we

Danielsen with his wife, Lina Niclasen.

had a refreshing time in the village. It was encouraging to hear the young in Christ speak of *Him*. The old judge was very happy in seeing some of his own children and townspeople won for the Saviour. He had long been praying and waiting for this, and now we rejoice together.

The gospel paper, *Naade og Sandhed* (Grace and Truth) which Br. Brend and I commenced last January, has been blessed of God. We have over seven hundred paying subscribers, while poor people get it free. The paper being in Danish, we have even subscribers in Denmark and Norway. We have had letters of thanks and testimonies that the periodical has been blessed to many souls, and has brightened many hearts and homes among the Faroe Islands. Many in these trying days are longing for that peace which the word cannot give, and there is much interest manifested in the gospel.

D. J. Danielsen[57]

Soon an assembly had come into existence at Søldarfjørður under the dynamic leadership of Victor Danielsen. D. J. Danielsen's health, however, was failing, and he had to make the journey by sea to Copenhagen for treatment in the better equipped hospitals there. He probably had some chronic systemic condition affecting his heart, for the doctors who had examined him prior to him going to the Congo had thought 'that there were some slight doubts as to his physical fitness for longer life'.[58]

Faroe Isles

Before going to Denmark for medical treatment, Mr. Danielsen had the joy of baptizing the first believers in the new assembly of Søldarfjørður, among them the young school-teacher whom God has so much used in that place, and an old lady of 72. A young widow was also baptized by him at Tórshavn having come from Suðuroy on purpose. Having been ill for months, he has been sorry to be unable to thank friends for their kind gifts.

Danielson's heart is affected and he was entering a hospital at Copenhagen for x-ray treatment. The doctors give hope of recovery, but he is very weak. He may be addressed c/o Mr. H. H. Hansen, Randersgade 16–4, Copenhagen O, Denmark, where his wife is staying.[59]

...

Mrs. Danielsen writes that several times her husband seemed about to breathe the last, but in answer to prayer he improved a little, and the doctor advised his returning home to the Faroe Isles, as nothing more could be done. They expect to leave Copenhagen early in October.[60]

However, the hopes of the doctors in Copenhagen proved to be illusory. He came back to Tórshavn with Lina after a protracted rough sea crossing from Denmark. Two days later, at the age of 45, he died on 16 October 1916. *Echoes of Service* carried the following obituary:

Fallen Asleep

Mr. Danielsen [*sic*] was a native of the Faroe Islands, but was for some years employed by the Congo Balolo Mission in an engineering capacity. Dr. and Mrs. Guinness esteemed him highly, but circumstances led to his return to the Faroe Islands in 1904, after his marriage. At that time there were no assemblies of believers except in Tórshavn,[61] although much seed sowing had been long carried by our brother Sloan. Mr. Danielsen henceforth devoted himself to gospel work in his native land.

He had suffered from fever in Africa, and the result of this, together with his experiences in the work, seem to have been the cause of his last illness. His heart became affected, and he went, with his wife, to Denmark for treatment. He almost passed away in the hospital there, but to the surprise of all, revived a little, and the doctors, being unable to do more for him, advised him to return home, as he greatly desired. The voyage occupied eleven days, and the weather was rough, so his condition rapidly deteriorated. The captain and officers did all they could for him, and a brother from Faroe, who was travelling by the same boat attended him night and day throughout the voyage. On arrival at Tórshavn he was carried to his home, and the first afternoon he was able to converse, seeming rather better. In the evening his mind wandered and from then he was only to converse for small moments. Early the second morning he said, "Take me by hand, for now I am ready." A moment or two later he said, "Behold, He cometh," lifted up his eyes and passed away.

A large company of friends, both from town and country, followed his body to the grave with twenty-four taking turns in bearing the coffin, while seven brethren bore testimony to his work and faithfulness to God, and the gospel was preached to the hundred present. Mrs. Danielsen is wonderfully sustained by God, but should be remembered in prayer.[62]

He was buried in Tórshavn, in what is now the old cemetery. On his head-stone is written:

Virkaði i Congo 1901–1903
Ein óræddur hermaður Harrans
['Served in the Congo 1901–03 / A fearless soldier of the Lord']

Roger Casement, Danielsen's former companion, and by now Sir Roger Case-ment, died only a couple of months before him. Casement had been involved in the Irish nationalist movement that sought liberation from British rule. During World War I, he sought to obtain German support for a rebellion in Ireland. Shortly before the Easter Rising in Dublin in 1916, Casement landed in Ireland and was arrested. He was subsequently convicted and executed for treason. Despite Conan Doyle's efforts to have him spared, he was hanged on 3 August 1916, aged 51, in Pentonville Prison, London, where he was buried. Later he was reinterred in Ireland where he is now considered a national hero.

Daniel Danielsen is buried beside his mother-in-law, who apparently came back to the Faroes some time after Danielsen and his wife. Unfortunately, there is virtually no material left behind by him in the Faeroes. The couple had no children. Lina left the Faroes for Scotland around 1920, where she married a butcher named John Smith. She died in 1937, aged 58 years old. Even in his own islands Daniel Danielsen was largely forgotten.

The stamp, issued by the Faroese Postal Service to mark the Casement report in 1904. It can be obtained from www.stamps.fo

CONCLUSION

The first edition of Mark Twain's *King Leopold's Soliloquy* was poorly received by the reading public and its sales were low. The reason is undoubtedly simple. It had no photographs. It was the second edition that had the famous montage of nine children with cut-hands. The pamphlet then became well-known and was widely read, and it this version which is now available on the Internet.[1] By contrast, Conan Doyle's *The Crime of the Congo* included the montage on the front page of the first edition. It sold 25,000 copies in the week it first appeared, was reprinted several times, and was quickly translated into several languages.[2]

The montage is still widely used at present. In 2003 the BBC broadcast an 110 minutes-long documentary, *White King, Red Rubber, Black Death*, about Leopold's Congo. It began by showing five photographs and dramatising them being taken. The first four of them are from the montage. As a result these photographs were probably seen by millions and the programme is available on the Internet.[3] But the documentary only mentioned Morel, and only one photographer of atrocity photos, Alice Harris. It has been the argument of this book that Danielsen was the principal contributor to the montage, which contained possibly the most famous images of the atrocities in the Congo Free State. It would seem that the cause of Congo reform is unthinkable without Danielsen, but in fact he has been forgotten.

Why was Danielsen forgotten?

Until recently, Ruth Slade has been the only subsequent historian that has even mentioned the role of Danielsen in the Congo Reform Campaign after his return to Britain in 1903. After noting that Casement had been accompanied during a good part of his tour of investigation by Danielson, she writes:

> Guinness was unsure of the wisdom of publication before the official report from Casement appeared, but after several weeks of persuasion it seemed to Morel that he was ready to cooperate, and Morel himself was convinced of the importance of the public interest which may thus be aroused, in its effect on the government. Morel wrote directly to Danielson, urging him to use his influence with Guinness, and stressing the importance of publicity and speed.

The CBM Council had been stirred to action after hearing the story Danielson had to tell them on his return to England, and at its meeting on 26 November decided to publish a booklet of missionary evidence on condition in the Congo State, and to arrange a series of mass meetings in the leading cities of England.[4]

The most recent history of the RBMU, *Drumbeats that Changed the World* (2000), fails to mention Danielsen. Although David Lagergren in *Mission and State in Congo* refers to the charges against Danielsen, and that the Mission took up those charges,[5] he fails to state that the Mission found Danielsen not guilty.[6] Only with the appearance of Dean Pavlakis's work on Congo reform will a historian give Danielsen his place in history. Perhaps less excusably, Danielsen's contemporaries were also subsequently silent on his role, and as we have seen, began editing him out even as events unfolded. From the end of 1903 neither Morel nor Guinness even mentioned Danielsen in anything they wrote about the Congo question. What could be the reasons for such omissions?

It is possible that social class might be an explanation. A feeling of racial and social superiority is apparent in John Harris's remark, in his letter quoted above in chapter 6, that 'to call the Director of a trading company "a drunken fool" to his face might do in Denmark but not on the Congo'. Grattan Guinness was truly a 'gentleman', coming from the famous brewery family with the same name, and the other key individuals, Casement, Morel, and Armstrong, would similarly be among the middle-classes, whilst Danielsen, being an engineer and coming from an unknown place in the world, was far from being by race, education, and employment was in a lower social class.

Dr. Neil Dickson has put this plausibly:

Given Guinness's sense of the need for caution, he may have been annoyed by Danielsen's impatience to get the campaign started. Guinness would undoubtedly feel that evangelism was the priority and would not want to do anything that would harm diplomatic relations with King Leopold which might lead to the expulsion of his missionaries (remember too that the Belgians were Catholics, while Guinness was running a Protestant mission). My feeling is that they all saw Danielsen as what the Americans would call 'a bit-player' i.e. a minor actor in the affair, while it was the middle-class individuals with the contacts in high places who make things happen, and, of course, they were right. Given the times, those with the social contacts would be more readily listened to.[7]

There are other possible explanations, however. At a meeting of the RBMU directors on 26 November 1903 the following was recorded:

> It was agreed with regard to Congo atrocities that a pamphlet should be prepared and published, if possible before Christmas, giving the missionary evidence on the terrible results of the present regime.
>
> The pamphlet should not be published by the RBMU but commercially as the author might arrange.
>
> It was also unanimously agreed that a number of meetings should be organized throughout Great Britain and Ireland, on this subject, and on the lines of the meeting recently held by the Acting Director at the Colston Hall, Bristol. Mr. Whytock's help should be employed with regard to meetings in Scotland, Mr. Pope's for the north of England, Mr. Wilkes' for the South and Mr. Talbot's for London arrangements. It was felt that at the present crisis of Congo affairs no better response could be made than the publication referred to and the meetings projected.
>
> With regard to Mr. Danielson it was decided that the Directors should await the recommendation of the Field Committee before taking any steps.[8]

This decision was also confirmed by the Congo Council later in the day. Danielsen is not even mentioned in connection with the planning of the campaign despite the fact that he already had started it, and having newly returned from the Congo, and having been in the company of Casement, he knew more than those in the RBMU in London of the reality of the situation there. Guinness was curiously reluctant to mention Danielsen in any public statements. Even as early as November 1903 in *Regions Beyond*, in an evident reference to Danielsen's activities, he only refers to having just received 'from one of our missionaries fresh evidence regard to recent atrocities.'[9] As far as we know from existing sources, this was the closest he came to referring to Danielsen in public.

In January 1904 the magazine had two articles about the Congo. One is written by Grattan Guinness, which so informative that the latter part of it is reproduced on page 116. In the article Guinness also prints, above the caption 'Maimed for Life', a photograph of a boy with a hand cut-off. The photograph must be one of those Danielsen brought home from the Congo in October 1903, and the accompanying history of the photograph is un-doubtedly from him, but there is no mention of him.

By the time Guinness wrote *Congo Slavery* in 1904, it was Casement's role as 'His Majesty's Consul' in exposing the atrocities that he mentions. In his

The Congo Crises of 1908 it is the Harrises he pays tribute to, but again there is no mention of Danielsen. Of course, one additional simple explanation of the omissions should not be overlooked. In a print dominated period, no-one at the time realized the significance photographs came to have or the importance of attributing them. That this changed is one further legacy of the CRA campaign.

Probably Guinness's silence has a further explanation. It is evident from the directors meeting of November 1903 that they were already considering a possible dismissal of Danielsen from the mission. As he had ignored the decision of the Congo Council to await the arrival of Casement before taking any steps, could that be the reason? In a letter, Morel had written to Danielsen on 17 November 1903:

> You will understand, of course that I don't want to go behind Dr. Grattan Guinness in any way, you must abide by the wishes of your chief, and would naturally do so; but I am convinced that we are allowing valuable time to elapse, and the grass to grow under our feet, by these delays. All the information that can be got should be published at once.[10]

Did Guinness have had the feeling that Danielsen was too inclined to act without following the direction of himself and the RMBU council? Certainly both Danielsen and Morel wanted something to happen right away, while Guinness was more cautious.

The minutes of the council meeting of 26 November concluded:

> Having received a communication from Mr. Gilchrist containing a quotation from a letter from Mr. Armstrong with reference to Danielson's utter unreliability of statement and suggesting that he be not sent to Congo again. His case was carefully reconsidered. After consideration the Council unanimously resolved that for the present we suspend our judgement on him as we cannot possibly reconcile the contradictory reports received about him.[11]

It is evident from this that Danielsen had not only had 'enemies' on the field. He had also supporters. Tensions among the missionaries were usually smoothed over for home consumption, but they are clear in the statements before the council. It took quite a long time before the Field Committee also took its definite decision. The letter from Armstrong was a clear attempt to damage the credibility of Danielsen. Earlier, Armstrong had described how useful Danielsen was to the mission and himself in *Regions Beyond*, both as engineer and as preacher when he 'kindly takes the morning service week about, and leaves my free to make excursions'.[12]

What had happened to change his opinion? According to Spelier's report, behind the incident he recorded was said to be rumour which had been sponsored by the CBM missionaries to the effect that the British State would drive away the Belgians to replace them with Englishmen, and that rubber work would be finished in a few months.[13] It was certainly not Armstrong who had excited the people against the Belgians, for as we have seen, he was critical of the Africans to the Belgians. It could have been Danielson. He knew the language and we know that he was quite excited of all he had seen on the expedition with Casement. He was in addition often impulsive in his behaviour, and we know

RED RUBBER

THE STORY OF THE RUBBER
SLAVE TRADE ON THE CONGO

THE CONGO SCALES.
The Weighing of the Soul in the Scales.
Adapted from the " Book of the Dead."
(By kind permission of Sir F. Carruthers Gould).

E. D. MOREL

Morel's most famous book Red Rubber with a "cut hand" and King Leopold on the weight.

he had spoken to the local people, for later in Britain he said that he had been asked by the people to report about their conditions. Was this the episode that was the reason for Armstrong's hostility to Danielsen? Whatever the case, it is probable that Danielsen was more politicised in his advocacy of the African. This is apparent in his newspaper statements once back in Britain, probably arrived at in discussions with Casement. Armstrong appears to have had a tendency to side with the European political establishment against the African. It may simply have been political differences in how to deal with the atrocities that made him make his accusation of 'utter unreliability of statement'.

We are left with speculation. Clearly there was some lack of sympathy among the majority of the missionaries to Danielsen, and undoubtedly some of this was created by Danielsen himself. This is perfectly clear from John Harris's letter of June 1903 in which he accuses Danielsen of ungentlemanly conduct, the mistreatment of his African workers, and unnecessary tensions with his missionary passengers. Danielsen could be impulsive and argumentative, as both Harris and Casement could testify. With the more restrained English missionary, some of this tension was undoubtedly due to a culture clash with the blunt-spoken Faroeman, for he was forthright in his opinions which he held strongly. But after all the factors that might have turned Harris and Armstrong against him are taken into account, there remains the fact that the others among his fellow engineers were opposed to his return. What we do know is that at the same council meeting of 26 November a letter was also read from Danielsen asking that a definite decision be given him as to the future intention of the council regarding him. A separation from the RBMU seemed inevitable. Danielsen's health had deteriorated in the Congo. He had also married, and what seemed to make a parting of the ways final is his being declared *persona non grata* by the Belgian authorities in the Congo. At the same time a new field of operations had opened from him the Faroes, and it is probable, given the contentious nature of his parting with the RBMU, that once he was out of sight, he was out of mind. Consequently, he was forgotten to history.

Real achievements

To turn from what must necessarily be speculation over the reasons for the neglect of Danielsen by his contemporaries, it has been the aim of his book to recall his very real achievements. The picture of Danielsen it has sought to portray has found support in the academic community. Kevin Grant, professor of History at Hamilton College and the author of *Civilised Savagery*, has written of the arguments put forward for Danielsen's photography, 'I'm persuaded by your argument that, given chronology and location, the source was more probably Danielson.'[14]

It is an extraordinary story of a young boy from some tiny, remote islands in the North Atlantic, who went abroad. When he came back some years later he had started a change in world history. After he died in 1916 he was a forgotten man. Nobody knew about his effort with regard to the Congo affairs, and after a while he was also almost forgotten for his missionary effort in the Faroes. He was not without his faults. But these often proved his strengths too. His passion for a cause, his impulse to throw himself wholeheartedly into it, and his desire to act rather than spectate were the qualities which made him what he was. Doubtless they could prove annoying to these of a more cautious, conservative nature who did not appreciate his outspoken manner. And doubtless some of the qualities which the English missionaries had found so off-putting, were ones that made him so thoroughly at home in his native Faroese culture and helped make him popular in the islands.

Danielsen was a man of the modern world in his readiness to embrace the new. Even Armstrong was ready to acknowledge his ability with machinery. But it is evident, too, in his love of the visual image which runs through his life like a thread. He realised the power of the photograph and brought back powerful ones from the Congo that were coveted by people such as E. D. Morel. Working in the Faroes, he remembered the advantages of the lantern slide show to spread his gospel message, and he continued to use the camera to supply the British missionary magazine, *Echoes of Service*, with images of the Faroes. The journal that he and Arthur Brend commenced in the islands was an early example of an illustrated publication in the islands. It is no surprise, then, that he found cartoon strips a temptation! He knew that a picture is worth a thousand words. It is to him, this book has argued, that we owe some of the most famous atrocity images from the Congo. As was noted, records of the provenance of photographs from the period is poor, and that Danielsen took the photographs has to be deduced from circumstantial evidence. He did not discover their use or invent the pose in the most famous of the atrocity ones, but it is entirely in character for someone who clearly had a strong visual sense that he should adopt them. His photography was to have a profound effect on the way in which subsequent humanitarian campaigns would be conducted.

There is no doubt that Danielsen anticipated important areas of the Congo Reform Campaign in 1903, from the time he met Casement and was engaged by him as an engineer and captain until he started the lantern lectures with photographs taken by himself. He pressed the Balolo Mission to be the first missionary society to follow up his campaign, and helped convince them. In the Faroes, too, he was an early mover among the islanders in the acceptance of the Brethren movement in which he played a significant part and which was to change his homeland. The results are the story of this book. It has brought to life forgotten history that should never die.

APPENDIX 1

Impongi

A famous atrocity photo is of Impongi, but very little is known of him.

In *Red Rubber* Morel printed the photo with the caption *Impongi, a boy of Illnega. Mutilated by State Soldiers.*[1] No photographer is mentioned. It was also reproduced in Morel's Special Congo supplement to the *West African Mail* of September 1905.[2] But *Regions Beyond* printed some news about Impongi much later on. The journal printed the same photo of Impongi with the following caption:

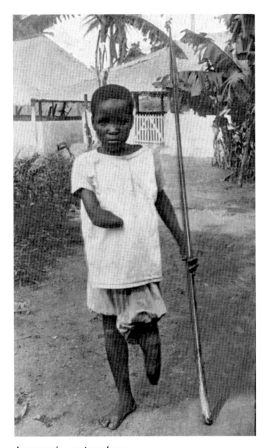

Impongi – a teacher.

Impongi – a teacher

In a recent letter from the Congo, the Rev. Charles Padfield, whilst touring amongst the villages near Ikau, writes: "I passed on to Ilinga and was conscious that preparatory work had been done there. By whom? You remember Impongi, the boy whose sad tale moved people's heart and whose photograph showing his hand and foot taken of convinced men of the reign of hell on the Congo – but it is he who taught these people the story of Redeeming Love."[3]

It seems that Impongi had taken up evangelistic and educational work. Also he does not come from Illnega as Morel wrote. He is from Ilinga, which is a village some 20 km from Ikau, where CBM had a mission station, and which

Impongi lived in the Ikau area. Here we see Ikau from the river.

Casement had visited in 1903. That shows once again that Morel was not very precise regarding exact facts in his publications. In February 1910 there was more news of Impongi:

From Ikau Mr. Padfield sends us a most heartening report. He writes:

   On Sunday it was our glad privilege to baptise thirty four. They were from the following places in our district: Waka, seven; Bokakata, six; Bobanga, seven, Lisifa, one; Ntombal, one; and the rest from Ikau. One special feature was that seven women then baptised were the wives of seven Church members. One other feature was the baptism of Impongi, the mutilated boy. It is worth recording that not one of the men and women baptised was received into Church Fellowship with greater heartiness. It as was a pathetic sight to see the poor lad coming up out of the water.[4]

Regions Beyond had a photograph of Impongi with his fellows, taken on the occasion:

You can see him passing up the pathway with the help of a stout stick. Impongi you will remember had a leg and a hand chopped off by the workmen of an India rubber agent, when they made a raid on a village because the miserable inhabitants had been unable to procure the excessive quantity of rubber demanded by

Impongi leaving the river after the baptism.

the White man. He is one of the many living monuments to the atrocious treatment meted out to the Congo natives by the official representatives of civilisation![5]

It is most interesting, that we now can locate Impongi to the Ikau area. That was the next mission station Casement visited after Bonginda. He visited Ikau up the Congo River on 27 and 28 August and down the river 4 and 5 September.

We know now that Danielsen may has been closer to Impongi than any other known photographer.

We also know that neither *Regions Beyond* nor Morel attributed any of Danielson's photographs. But we also know that Harris had in his lantern slides a photograph called *'The boy Impongi. Mutilated wantonly.'* It could be the same photograph.

APPENDIX 2

Bokwala

In 1910 The Religious Tract Society published the book *Bokwala—The story of a Congo victim* with a preface of H. Grattan Guinness. The book was said to be an unknown moving voice from a victim of Leopold's regime. It was advertised in *Regions Beyond* to be the 'Uncle Tom's Cabin of the Congo'. The book is available as an e-text on the Internet as a free download.[1]

No author was mentioned in the book, although it has a foreword by Dr. Harry Grattan Guinness; historians have concluded, that Bokwala was a fictitious person, and that the book is a fiction. There could be no doubt that the text had been written by an English-speaking missionary, but as it was not known who this individual was. The tract is probably based on a template created by slave-trade abolitionists. It is known that some abolitionist tracts which were written in the voice of a slave were not actually written by slaves. Both the abolitionists and the Congo reformers wanted to move people to action by what they wrote, and if invented stories could assist, they were happy to use them. That Bokwala is fictitious is also admitted in *Regions Beyond* by the CBM missionary William Wilkes: 'Although, perhaps, all the incidents recorded did not actually happen in the experience of one person, yet every incident mentioned is an historical fact. To quote the words of the Author, Bokwala's story is the truth, and nothing by the truth.'[2]

During the research for this book, the author was discovered. In the minutes of the meeting of the Congo Council 16 November 1909 it was reported that Mrs. Ruskin, a missionary of the Congo Balolo Mission, had sent home material for the book. She was working at Bongindanga up the river from Bonginda, Danielsen's station. According to the minute book, the question arose as to whether the fees for the copyright and other probable payment should be the property of the author or of the mission. It was agreed, that the fees should be the property of the mission, but that the author should receive an honorarium which was later agreed as £20. That indicates that the Balolo Mission supported the book and was involved in its publication.

Lily and Edward Algernon Ruskin were working at the CBM mission station in Bongandanga, the most distant of the stations Casement visited in 1903. They were linguists and much involved with translations of the Bible.

Their colleague at the station Mr. Jeffrey wrote in 1905: 'Mr. and Mrs. Ruskin are our best linguists. Mrs. Ruskin has an excellent memory, and as she goes into the villages and hears a new word, she can keep it in memory without writing it down.'[3] The Ruskins also wrote a grammar of the Lomóngo language, also called Mongo. Mongo speakers reside in central DR Congo over a large area inside the curve of the Congo River. Lily Ruskin wrote other publications about the Congo. Probably the linguistic work has brought her into closer contact with the people than other missionaries. Mrs. Ruskin had had rich possibilities when speaking to people to obtain their histories.

The fictitious character of Bokwala was the son of a chief. His experiences while all known to have happened in the Congo are unlikely to have all happened to one man. A few extracts from the book will be reproduced here:

Experiencing the chicotte:
When the day came for carrying my basket to the white man I had not the prescribed quantity. I knew that when my turn came to have my rubber weighed the white man would be angry and scold me, but said I "Lotango nta a wak'ontu" (Reproach does not kill a man), and I did not expect anything worse.

But the order was given, "Etama" (Lie down).

I could scarcely believe my ears – I, the son of a chief, to be whipped publicly!

It was true. I was placed face down on the ground, my cloth turned back, and the twisted hippo hide whip was brought out by one of the servants of the white man.

Down it came on me, lash after lash, cutting clean into the flesh at every stroke, and causing to blood to flow!

I do not know how many strokes were given me then; how could I count? The pain was bad enough, but the shame was worse. Then I was sent off, the blood drops on the sand showing the path I followed, without payment for the rubber I had brought, and with order to bring a double quantity next time.[4]

Women hostages:
In a village not far from my father's the men were all away on one occasion trying to procure what was required of them as their weekly tax.

When the day for bringing it in fell due, they did not arrive in good time, and as usual sentries were sent out to inquire into it.

Finding no men in town, and most of the women having fled into the bush in fear at the approach of the sentries, they seized the wife of one of the absent men. She had recently become a mother; perhaps she was not strong enough to run away with her companions. Anyway she was arrested with her babe at her breast, and taken off to the white man's place, where it was decided to give the village a lesson that they would not soon forget.

In the presence of the white man the poor thing was stretched on the ground, and the awful hippo-hide whip was brought into requisition.

The man who started the whipping became tired, and passed the whip over to another to continue it, until at last, when the woman was more dead than alive, and in a condition which cannot be described to you, the white man gave the order to cease, and she was — set free, did you say? — No, sent into the prison house!

An hour or two later her husband arrived and was told that if he wanted to redeem his wife he must bring the white man twenty fowls. He succeeded in collecting sixteen, which were refused, then he made up the number, and so redeemed his wife and babe. This redemption must have cost him a great deal of money, and he was a poor man.

Three days after her return to her home the wife died.[5]

The conclusion: Things We Want to Know

WHITE men of Europe, my story is finished. I have told you about the past, and the two kinds of slavery in which we have been bound; I have told you about the present, our constant work, the difficulty in which our chiefs find themselves placed, our inability to marry because of our poverty, our sickness, the desolation which broods over our villages, the lack of children to take the places of those who die. I think I have told you sufficient to show you that we are in need of pity and help.

I want to ask you, white people of Europe, two questions. The first is, "Why are these things so?"

Long ago, our fathers tell us and some of us can remember, there were no white people in our land; we lived alone and happily in our own way. True, there were feuds and fights, quarrels and bloodshed, and a kind of slavery, but the country was ours, the forest was ours in which to hunt, the river was ours in which to fish, the fruits of the forest and the produce of our gardens were ours to appease our hunger. We did not know anything about white men, nor did we wish to.

And then — suddenly they came in their steamers and settled amongst us. And gradually we learnt that these white men, who came to us uninvited, are our masters — we, our families, our forests, the produce of our gardens, the spoil of our hunting and fishing — all belong to them. And we cannot understand why it should be so.

Once more, we have to work for the white man all the time. Now, when the work is lighter than ever, we are in the forest two out of every three months. We must get a certain quantity of rubber, or there is prison for us, and, when we come out of prison, more rubber must be made in place of what was short before we can make a start on the next three-monthly portion.

Those of us who are taking food are out on the river fishing from the first to the fifth working day, and we take in the food on the sixth. If we hunt, we must be continually going to the forest, which is not any better. The food-tax men are worse off than the rubber men at present. For all this constant work we receive very little pay, and, if we complain, we are told that all this work is "wuta" ("tax"). We knew about "wuta" long ago before the white men came, but our „wuta" was to pass over a part of what we had in consideration of some benefit received, or the use of some implement, or in order to be freed from some obligation, but we never understood it to mean all that we had or anything which would take all our time.

Now, everything else has to be let go in order to get "wuta" for Bula Matadi, and I would ask you white men, Why is it so?

I have only one more question to ask you. It is this, for how long will it last?

Bokwala.

We were young men when it commenced, now we are middle-aged, and we seem no nearer to the end of it than we were at first. Still there is the demand for rubber, rubber, rubber.

Many of our people have died from exposure to cold and heat, or from lack of comfort; many others from accidents, such as falling from the rubber vines, and many more from the pestilences of which I have told you.

White men, I tell you the truth: we are dying, soon our villages will be put out as a fire that is quenched.

And still we are working, still we are slaves to the white men.

And we have nothing to look forward to, as far as we can see, except constant work — and death. We have heard that when a man reaches what the white men call forty years of age his tax palaver is finished; but that time must be in very old age, for no one ever seems to become old enough to leave off work.

No, the only rest we can look forward to is death!

The white men of God are still with us, and they still tell us the news of salvation from sin.

That is good news.

But again I say that what we want to hear is the news of salvation from rubber. How long before we shall hear that news? How long a time must pass before this "wuta" business is finished? How long shall we wait before we get a little rest — apart from death?[6]

This message to the 'white men' in 1909, is similar to the message Danielsen in 1903 brought from the people in Congo, as seen in the articles in the *West African Mail* and *Daily Record and Mail*, printed in Chapter 5. *Bokwala* shows the continuing attention of the CBM to the situation in the Congo. It also illustrates that as late as 1909, when the book was written not much had changed for local people.

Bokwala has until now been dismissed by historians as a famous fraud. However now properly attributed it can be reassessed as a late piece

Algernon and Lily Ruskin and two African boys. The standing boy helped Mr. Ruskin to learn the language.

of missionary propaganda in the long campaign for reform in the Congo. It is also another part of the history of the Congo Balolo Mission, which not has been known until now.

ABBREVIATIONS IN NOTES

CBM – Congo Balolo Mission
CBMM1 – Executive Committee minutes of Congo Balolo Mission
CBMM2 – Standing Committee minutes of Congo Balolo Mission
CRA – Congo Reform Association
EDMP – E. D. Morel papers
EoS – Echoes of Service
RB – Regions Beyond

NOTES

NOTES TO PREFACE

1. 'Danielsen' is the correct Faroese spelling of the name however most sources in English refer to him as 'Danielson'. I have kept the original spelling in any sources reproduced here.
2. Sigurd Berghamar, *...men Gud gav vøkst* (Tórshavn, 1992), 220.
3. Jens av Reyni, *Vejen* (Tórshavn, 1941), 5–6.
4. Óli Jacobsen, *Dollin: Havnarmaðurin sum broytti heimssøguna* [*Dollin: The Faroese who changed history in the Congo*] (Tórshavn, 2010). To allow non-Faroese speakers access to Danielsen's story, the book has a detailed summary in English and the captions for illustrations are also in English.
5. An online archive of its previous papers is available at 'Brethren Archivists and Historians Network' <http://www.brethrenhistory.org/>.
6. University of Edinburgh, Centre for the Study of Christianity in the Non-Western World, Regions Beyond Missionary Union Archive, CSCNWW33, Congo Balolo Mission Minutes [hereafter CBMM1].
7. University of Edinburgh, Centre for the Study of Christianity in the Non-Western World, Regions Beyond Missionary Union Archive, CSCNWW33, Congo Balolo Mission Minutes [hereafter CBMM2].
8. London School of Economics, E. D. Morel papers, MOREL/F1-18 [hereafter EDMP].
9. It is only by chance that these letters are available. The archive was located by an American research student at Morel's son's farm. They were brought to British Library and London School of Economics. David Issacson, called my attention to the documents first in 2010.

10. *Africa No. 1 (1904). Correspondence and Report from His Majesty's Consul at Boma Respecting the Independent State of the Congo* (London, 1933) [online text] <https://archive.org/details/CasementReport>, accessed 7 Mar. 2014.
11. Séamas Ó Síocháin and Michael O'Sullivan (eds.), *The Eyes of Another Race: Roger Casement's Congo Report and 1903 Diary* (Dublin, 2003), 167–72.

NOTES TO CHAP. 1: THE MAKING OF A MISSIONARY

1. There was a tradition within her family that the most famous visitor to one house in which she was in service was Hans Christian Andersen.
2. Tórður Jóansson, *Brethren in the Faroes: An Evangelical Movement, its Remarkable Growth and Lasting Impact in a Remote Island Community* (Tórshavn, 2012), 70.
3. A brief account of the Faroes can be found in Tórður Jóansson, 'The Brethren in the Faeroes: Some Contexts for Growth', *Brethren Historical Review*, vol. 6 (2010), 54–73; the standard history in English is John West: *Faroe: The Emergence of a Nation* (London, 1972).
4. Óli Jacobsen, ' *"Gamli Sloan"*: William Gibson Sloan after 175 Years', *Brethren Historical Review*, vol. 9 (2013), 10–19.
5. CBMM1, 76th Congo Council, 28 Feb. 1901.
6. Ibid.
7. However, the editors of *Echoes of Service*, in a note prefacing one of Danielsen's letters, evidently relying on information supplied by Danielsen, state he was converted in 1897. This is clearly either a slip on Danielsen's part, or a misreading of Danielsen's letter by the editors, or a printers' error, as CBMM1, 76th Congo Council, 28 Feb. 1901, gives his age as 29 and states that Danielsen 'has only been a Christian for eighteen months'. As Danielsen elsewhere gave his age at conversion as 27 (*Naade og Sandhed*, May 1917, 41–4.), this would seem to place his conversion in the spring of 1898, before his birthday in that year.
8. As Alexander Galbraith, a prominent leader in revivalist circles in Glasgow, was the principal individual in the Christian meeting through which Danielson was converted, most probably Danielson was converted through the Seamen's Bethel in Eaglesham St., Glasgow, which was a member of the Glasgow Evangelistic Association, a federation of mission halls. Mission halls had a similar ethos to the Brethren, but maintained closer links with the institutional church and leaving a denomination was not a prerequisite of membership.
9. After Danielsen's death in 1916, his fellow evangelist, Arthur Brend, wrote: 'After having served the seamen's mission he offered the Balolo Mission his service. He went then to London and spent a year's time at Harley, where he prepared for his missionary service in inner Africa, where he served for three years' (*Naade og*

Sandhed, No. 11, Nov. 1916). The statement that Danielsen spent a year at Harley College after his conversion is repeated in Danielsen's obituary in *Dimmalætting*, 18 Oct. 1916, and undoubtedly Brend is again the source. As well as the evident inaccuracies in Brend's obituary, this chronology is also hard to square with that given by the editors of *Echoes of Service* which had Danielsen as its source. According to it, Danielsen was in South Africa 'for some time' and it was there 'he answered an advertisement for a Christian engineer for the Congo' (*EoS* (1905), 184, quoted on 128). In addition, when Danielsen was accepted for the CBM, no mention was made of a period at Harley College, nor were character references taken from anyone associated with it (CBMM1, 76th Congo Council, 28 Feb. 1901), which would be an astonishing omission, given the close association through the Guinnesses of Harley and the CBM. The chronology followed in the text accepts contemporary and earlier sources as the more reliable.

10. Danielsen family papers, A. W. Sloan, 'D. J. Danielsen, trúboðari [missionary] / F. 25. Juni 1871 / D. 18. Oktob. 1916 / Fyrsti føroyski "heidningamissionerur" [The first Faeroese "missionary to the heathen"]', unpublished MS, n.d.; it is Sloan who cites Galbraith as the leading individual in the Glasgow meeting (see Chap.1, n.8 above).

11. CBMM1, 76th Congo Council, 28 Feb. 1901.

12. *EoS*, vol. 33 (1904), p 184.

13. Livingstone worked in Africa for 30 years before his death. On his last trip he was funded by the Royal Geographic Society in an attempt to find the source of the Nile. It was during this trip that his famous meeting with H. M. Stanley occurred. Livingstone died during this trip, thinking that he had found the source of the Nile in the Lualaba River. In fact Stanley would prove that this was the source of the Congo River.

14. Faith missions were so-called because of their stress on 'living by faith'. However, Klaus Fiedler argues that their interdenominational characteristics were of greater importance in defining them. He defines them in historical context as 'a mission which traces its origin or (more often) the origin of its principles directly or indirectly back to the China Inland Mission': *Klaus Fielder, The Story of Faith Missions: From Hudson Taylor to Present Day Africa* (Carlisle: 1994), 11.

15. Joseph F. Conley, *Drumbeats that Changed the World: A History of the Regions Beyond Missionary Union and the West Indies 1873–1999* (Pasadena, CA: 2000), 39. Conley remarks that this policy meant that EDL trained people were present throughout many Protestant missionary organisations. A brief history of the CBM can be found at <http://en.wikipedia.org/wiki/Congo-Balolo_Mission>, accessed October 2012; cf., Matthew Doherty, 'The Congo Balolo Mission and the Indigenous Christian Community: The Agency of Locals', in Amanda Bar-

ry *et al.* (eds), *Evangelists of Empire?: Missionaries in Colonial History*, [online text] Melbourne: University of Melbourne Scholarship Research Centre, 2008, <http://msp.esrc.unimelb.edu.au/shs/missions>, accessed October 2012.

16. Conley, *Drumbeats*, 101–2, 499 n.215. In 1991 the RBMU merged with the Evangelical Union of South America to form Latin Link.

17. CBMM1, 76th Congo Council 28th February 1901. The full minute reads: 'Mr. Danielson – The application of Mr. Danielson for service in the Engineering Department was fully considered, and he was interviewed by the Council. He is 29 years of age, and is a native of the Faroe Islands. The whole of his engineering and marine experience hitherto has been in connection with Scotch firms. All his certificates of discharge from the various vessels in which he has sailed are marked 'very good' both for conduct and acuity. Although he has only been a Christian for eighteen months, he has not, previous to his conversion been under the power of vicious habits, and his referees speak of him as a 'thoroughgoing Christian and one who is afraid of nothing in his Masters work'. Mr. Danielson had been medically examined by Dr. [name indistinct] and Mr. Eccles and it appeared that there were some slight doubts as to his physical fitness for longer life. As however he had had practical experience and had never suffered in any way the Council felt they ought to accept Mr. Danielson's offer, and he was, therefore, unanimously accepted on the mentions of Mr. Cory seconded by Mr. Brown. Mr. Eccles desired that it should be recorded in the minutes as to the slight doubt that existed from the health stand point.'

18. For this chronology, see above, Chap. 1, n.9.

19. CBMM1, List of Congo Missionaries until 1909.

20. Conley, *Drumbeats*, 91; *RB*, Aug.–Sept. 1909, also credits Mr. and Mrs. Gamman for the translation and the printing of the New Testament.

21. Ruth Slade, 'English Missionaries and the Beginning of the Anti-Congolese Campaign in England', *Revue belge de philologie et d'histoire*, 33/1 (1955), 37–73, 40.

22. Ibid.

23. CBMM1, 28 Feb. 1901.

24. *RB* Jan.–Feb. 1908, 52.

25. CBMM1, 29 May 1901.

26. *RB* (June 1902), 179.

27. CBMM2, 10 and 12 May 1902.

28. CBMM1, 30 Oct. 1902.

29. The word 'palaver' is an interesting one in the 40 west African context. It was a process whereby a problem was fully discussed and some form of a consensus was reached to resolve the problem. The missionary was often called on to oversee 'palavers'. His or her place was to stand as judge but also as a sort of

impartial negotiator. For a definition of the modern palaver see Marguerite A. Peeters, 'The African Palaver Tradition and the Western Postmodern Consensus: Convergences and Divergences', Dialogue Dynamics, 2009, <http://www.dialoguedynamics.com/content/learning-forum/modules/consensus-palabre/article/the-african-palavertradition-and> accessed 20 Feb. 2014.

30. *RB* (1902), 279.
31. *RB* (1901), 309.
32. *RB* (1903), 207.
33. Sloan, 'D. J. Danielsen, trúboðari' unpublished MS.
34. H. Grattan Guinness: *"Not unto us:" A Record of Twenty-One Years' Missionary Service* (London, 1908), 75.
35. Sloan, 'D. J. Danielsen, trúboðari', unpublished MS.

NOTES TO CHAP. 2: SERIOUS ACCUSATIONS

1. Lloyd A. Cooke, 'Terence B. Sawyers' in 'Dictionary of African Christian Biography', <http://www.dacb.org/stories/ghana/sawyers-terence.html>, accessed 5 October 2014. Cook notes that T. B. Sawyers probably worked for the Guinness mission in the Congo before becoming associated, as an ordained minister, with Baptist churches in Jamaica. I am grateful to Dr Dean Pavlakis for drawing my attention to this probable identification.
2. George Washington William, quoted in; Adam Hochschild, *King Leopold's Ghost: A Story of Greed, Terror, and Heroism in Colonial Africa* (Boston, 1998), p.112.
3. CBMM1, 26 March 1903.
4. CBMM1, 28 May 1903.
5. CBMM2, minutes of meeting of the held at Ikau on the 1st, 2nd and 3rd June 1903.
6. CBMM1 24th June 1903.
7. CBMM2, 24 September 1903.

NOTES TO CHAP. 3: CASEMENT'S COMPANION

1. Wm. Roger Louis and Jean Stengers (eds.), *E. D. Morel's History of the Congo Reform Movement* (Oxford, 1968), ix.
2. *The West African Mail* went bankrupt in 1907 and so Morel launched the *African Mail*.
3. Adam Hochschild, *King Leopold's Ghost: A Story of Greed, Terror, and Heroism in Colonial Africa* (Boston, 1998), 189–91.
4. Ibid., 190.

5. Ruth M. Slade: 'English-speaking Missions in the Congo Independent State, 1878-1908', thesis, Bruxelles, 1959, 275.

6. Letter from Roger Casement to the Foreign Secretary, London, 13 Oct. 1903, National Archives, Kew Gardens.

7. Roger Casement, 1903 Diary entry, 17 July, in Ó Síocháin and O'Sullivan (eds.), *Eyes of Another Race*, 247.

8. Ó Síocháin and O'Sullivan (eds.), *Eyes of Another Race*, 49–177.

9. Ibid., 167–72.

10. Roger Casement, 1903 Diary, 5 July and 28 August, in Ó Síocháin and O'Sullivan (eds.), *Eyes Another Race*, 258, 261.

11. *Africa No. 1 (1904)*, [online text], 43.

12. Slade, 'English-speaking Missions', 276.

13. Ó Síocháin and O'Sullivan (eds.), *The Eyes of Another Race*, 251.

14. Roger Casement, 1903 Diary, 30 August, Ó Síocháin and O'Sullivan (eds.), *Eyes of Another Race*, 254

15. Ibid., 264.

16. Ibid.

17. David Lagergren: *Mission and State in the Congo. A Study of the Relations between Protestant Missions and the Congo Independent State Authorities with Special Reference to the Equator District, 1885–1903*, trans. Owen N. Lee (Lund, 1970), 334, 335.

18. Roger Casement, 1903 Diary, 12 Dec., in Ó Síocháin and Michael O'Sullivan (eds.), *Eyes of Another Race*, 291.

19. Séamas Ó Síocháin e-mail to the writer. I had regular contact with Séamas Ó Síocháin, a lecturer at the National University of Ireland, Maynooth, while writing my biography. The editorial material of *The Eyes of Another Race* confirms this assessment of Danielsen's role.

20. Roger Casement, 1903 Diary, 25 and 28 July, Ó Síocháin and O'Sullivan (eds.), *Eyes of Another Race*, 249

21. Roger Casement to the Foreign Secretary, 13 October 1903, National Archives, Kew.

NOTES TO CHAP. 4: BACK IN BRITAIN

1. 15 September, in Ó Síocháin and O'Sullivan (eds.), *Eyes of Another Race*, 269.

2. EDMP, H. Grattan Guinness to E. D. Morel, 16 Oct. 1903.

3. CBMM1, 22 Oct. 1903.

4. CBMM1, 24 June 1896.

5. *RB*, April 1903, 134.

6. Ibid.
7. Séamas Ó Síocháin and Michael O'Sullivan, 'General Introduction', in *idem* (eds.), *Eyes of Another Race*, 6–7.
8. CBMM1, 24 Sept. 1896; in fact there were three RC missionaries investigating.
9. Lagergren, *Mission and State in the Congo*, 267. It is perhaps unfair to describe Guinness as the best exemplar of the appeased missionary. Although he certainly showed favour for Leopold's regime, the Baptist Missionary Society was undoubtedly more closely courted and less supportive of the later reform campaign.
10. EDMP, H. Grattan Guinness to E. D. Morel, 17 Oct. 1902.
11. Kevin Grant, *A Civilised Savagery: Britain and the New Slaveries in Africa, 1884–1926* (New York & London, 2005), 51; Conley, *Drumbeats*, 84, gives a similar explanation for Guinness's initial silence.
12. Louis and Stengers (eds.), *E. D. Morel's History*, 106–7.
13. CBMM1, 5 Feb. 1903.
14. Ibid, 26 Feb. 1903.
15. *RB*, Apr. 1903, 131–136.
16. Cf. the identical conclusion for the silence of the missionaries in the quotation from Grant, *A Civilised Savagery*, and from Conley, *Drumbeats*, at n.11 above.
17. *RB*, April 1903, 131–6, quotation 132.
18. Louis and Stengers (eds.), *E. D. Morel's History*, 270.
19. Ibid., 270.
20. Grant, *A Civilised Savagery*, 51.
21. The CRA meetings often ran at a loss. For more detail on finance, see Pavlakis, *British Humanitarianism* (forthcoming).
22. T. Jack Thompson: *Light on Darkness? Missionary Photography of Africa in the Nineteenth and Early Twentieth Centuries* (Grand Rapids, MI, 2012), 1–2.
23. EDMP, H. Grattan Guinnes to E. D. Morel, 16 Oct. 1903.
24. EDMP, F10/8, Letter Book, f437-439, Edmund Morel to H. [*sic*] J. Danielson, 17 November 1903; the truth of Morel's observation can be seen in the absence of reports of Danielson's meetings of late 1903 in the Edinburgh press; the first note of agitation over the Congo in the Edinburgh newspaper, *The Scotsman*, was on 2 Feb. 1904, 4i, by which time the campaign had moved to Glasgow.

NOTES TO CHAP. 5: PRESS ATTENTION

1. EDMP, CA3225, *West African Mail*, 27 Nov. 1903.
2. *Daily Mirror*, 7 Dec. 1903, 1 col. iv.
3. Cf. 'I will tell everyone I can of this terrible slavery which is carried out in the Congo State. If this atrocious Administration goes on much longer, in a few

years' time whole districts will have become entirely and absolutely depopulated. Then Europe will awake. But it will be too late.'

4. EDMP, E. D. Morel to D. J. Danielson, 14 Dec. 1903.

5. 5 December and 7 December, Ó Síocháin and O'Sullivan (eds.), *The Eyes*, 292.

6. EDMP, D. J. Danielson to E. D. Morel, 4 Dec. 1903.

7. EDMP, E. D. Morel to Roger Casement 4 Dec. 1903.

8. It is possible that Reuters had put two and two together in its report, connecting the British consul of the Glasgow article with the D. J. Danielson of the *West African News* article, who had therefore become 'an Englishman' that had accompanied Casement in the Reuters' report.

9. *Daily Record and Mail*, Sat. 28 Nov. 1903, 1 col. i.

10. 'Grove Christian Centre: History', <https://sites.google.com/site/grovechristiancentre/history>, accessed 23 May 2014.

11. *Daily Record and Mail*, Mon. 30 Nov. 1903, 3 col. vii.

12. *Daily Record and Mail*, Tues. 1 Dec. 1903, 3 col. iii; Hochschild, *King Leopold's Ghost*, x. agrees with this assessment of the governance of the Congo on the prevalence of sleeping sickness.

13. *Tingakrossur*, 9 Mar. 1904.

14. *West African Mail*, 11 Dec. 1903, quoted in Jacobsen, Dollin, 191–2; *Falkirk Herald and Midlands County Journal*, 2 December, 6 col. ii.

NOTES TO CHAP. 6: A FORGOTTEN HERO

1. CBMM1, 6 November 1903.

2. Henry Fox Bourne to E. D. Morel 24 November 1903, quoted in Slade, 'English Missionaries', 69.

3. E. D. Morel to Herbert Ward, 10 November 1903: EDMP, F10, quoted in Slade, 'English Missionaries', 69.

4. *Africa No. 1 (1904). Correspondence and Report from His Majesty's Consul at Boma Respecting the Independent State of the Congo* (London, 1933), 63 [online text] <https://archive.org/details/CasementReport>, accessed 26 June 2014.

5. Morel to Ward, 10 November 1903, quoted in Slade, 'English Missionaries', 68.

6. CBMM1, 26 Nov. 1903.

7. EDMP, F5/3, E. D. Morel to D. J. Danielsen, 16 Dec. 1903.

8. EDMP, F5/3, D. J. Danielson to E. D. Morel, 22 Dec. 1903, reproduced in facsimile in Jacobsen, *Dollin*, 78–9.

9. John Harris to the Standing Committee (local committee of missionaries on the Congo), 23 Jun. 1903, Brit. Emp. S19 D5/7 54-58. Anti-Slavery archives at the

Bodleian Library of Imperial and Commonwealth Studies at Rhodes House. My thanks to Dr Dean Paklakis for sharing this source.

10. CBMM1, 26 Jan. 1904.
11. CBMM1, 22 Mar. 1904.
12. Belgian government on the Casement Report. <https://archive.org/details/CasementReport> accessed 29/07/2014. 54/86, 15.
13. CBMM1, 17 May 1904.
14. CBMM1, 14 Jun. 1904.
15. EDMP, E.D. Morel to D. J. Danielson, 4 Dec. 1903.
16. Ibid., 6 Oct. 1904.
17. CBMM1, 15 June 1905.

NOTES TO CHAP. 7: CONGO REFORM ASSOCIATION

1. EDMP, Roger Casement to E. D. Morel, 25 January 1904.
2. Louis and Stengers (eds.), *E. D. Morel's History*, 166.
3. Thompson, *Light on Darkness?*, 17.
4. Conley, *Drumbeats*, 87.
5. Hochshild, *King Leopold's Ghost*, 216.
6. *Ibid.*, 273–4.
7. Mark Twain, *King Leopold's Soliloquy: A Defence of His Congo Rule* (Boston, 1905), 5.
8. Twain, *Leopold's Soliloquy*, 40. Twain's pamphlet was itself illustrated with photographs. These were probably provided to him by Morel himself although they were taken by missionaries.
9. Hochschild, *King Leopold's Ghost*, 248.
10. At least some of the content of the article had already been published in the Faroese newspaper *Tingakrossur* in 18 Oct. 1905, more than a year before it was published in the USA! *Tingakrossur* was edited by my grandmother's cousin, Kristin Holm Isaksen, a fearless fighter against all kinds of injustice. He had already published on 16 Aug. 1903 an article about the cruelties in the Congo based on reports from Fox Bourne. Here is a section which was very similar: 'The people were killed by hanging, spearing, cutting the throat, but mostly with the rifle. Some of the women were tortured to death by forcing a pointed stake through the vagina into the womb. I knew of other such instances but in order to test him I asked him for an example. 'They killed my daughter Nsinga in this manner; I found the stake in her.' He told me of many other instances of terrible brutality, torture and murder, but I will not write them, not because there is any lack of proof (there is only too much), but because people in Europe would

absolutely refuse to believe that anyone could be so inhuman as to commit such acts.' It is clear from this that the incendiary nature of the material was present in the international press.

11. Mac Mckinney, 'The Pen Proves Mightier than the Chicotte: Full Scale War', *LA Progressive*, 12 June 2012.

12. Anon., *An Answer to Mark Twain* (Brussels, [1907]).

13. Ó Síocháin and O'Sullivan state in *The Eyes of Another Race*, 37: 'the judge Giovanno had succeded in getting Epondo to retract his story, a retraction confirmed … by Rev. Ellsworth Faris. The boy had lost his hand through gangrene following a bite from a wild pig.' However, in a personal communication Séamas Ó Síocháin stated to me he was not sure which version of Epondo's maiming contained the truth.

14. Extracts of Bosco's report are included on a collection of notes from the Belgian government on the Casement Report. <https://archive.org/details/CasementReport> accessed 29/07/2014. 54/86, 15. This puts Bosco in the area in September, the month after Casement left.

15. Ibid.

16. Ibid., 54/86, 16.

17. Ibid., 55/86, 17.

18. Ibid. The statement is not out of line with what is known of Armstrong's thoughts about Africans. Why Armstrong is giving a statement is not explained in Bosco's report, but as both Epondo and Armstrong were in Bonginda this is probably why he comments on this specific case.

19. *An Answer to Mark Twain*, 43

20. Leopold's Commission of Inquiry, 49

21. *RB*, 1905, 5.

22. *RB*, 1905, 77.

23. *RB*, March 1905, 80

24. Ibid.

25. Ibid.

26. *RB*, December 1905, 320.

27. Arthur Conan Doyle, *The Crime of Congo* (London [1909]), 53.

28. Hochschild, *King Leopold's Ghost*, 250.

29. In May 1906 Guinness concluded: 'When in December 1904, the Commission reached that part of the Congo State, Mr. Harris and Mr. Stannard brought hundreds of these unhappy people to give their testimony – and they gave it believing that these white men were their friends. But with what result? In Europe we know that not a single word of the native testimony was published in the long delayed report.' (*RB*, 1906, 112.)

30. R.C.T., 'What Britain Demands, *RB* (Dec., 1909), 204.

31. CBMM1, 13 Jul. 1909.

32. *RB*, December 1908, 229.

33. CBMM1, 4 Oct. 1910.

34. Hoschshild, *King Leopold's Ghost*, 274

35. Ibid., 278–9.

36. Ibid., 277.

37. Pavlakis, *British Humanitarianism and the Congo Reform Movement, 1896-1913* (Farnham, Surrey, forthcoming).

38. Ibid.

NOTES TO CHAP. 8: EVANGELICALS, ATROCITY PHOTOGRAPHS, AND DANIELSEN

1. Sharon Sliwinski, 'The Childhood of Human Rights: The Kodak on the Congo', Journal of Visual Culture, vol. 5/3 (December 2006), 334, 338, 340 <http://tps.jkdweb.biz/sites/default/files/uploads/Sliwinski_Kodak_Congo.pdf>, accessed October 2012. 334.

2. Anti-slavery International was formerly the Aborigines Protection Society. Many of the captions which have so far been attached to these photographs are incorrect. For example many of them are attributed to Alice Seeley Harris although they were taken in the period before she was known to be actively taking atrocity photographs.

3. David van Reybrouck, *Congo: The Epic History of a People* (2010), tr. Sam Garrett (New York, 2014), 99.

4. Edmund D. Morel, *Affairs of West Africa* (London, 1902), 335 [online text] <https://archive.org/stream/affairsofwestafr00more#page/334/mode/2up>.

5. 'I did in this volume … make King Leopold 'personally' responsible for the state of affairs in the Congo. It seemed to me that the time had come when the charge should be openly proffered and the blame placed on the right shoulders', Morel, *History of the Congo Reform Movement*, 98.

6. Morel claimed the boy was now cared for by English missionaries, but it is likely that he was in the care of the ABMU.

7. Interestingly there is evidence that Morel knew details of Mola Ekulite in 1902. In *Affairs of West Africa* he refers to a photograph of three figures. Later in *King Leopold's Rule* he refers to the same picture, naming one of the figures as Ekulite. Apparently this picture was never published as it was too blurred.

8. Sjöblom had gone to the Congo with the CBM, but was working the ABMU from 1893 untill his death in 1903. Morel re-publishes his testimony in: E. D.

Morel, *The Treatment of Women and Children in the Congo State. (1895-1904): An Appeal to the Women of the United States of America* (Boston, 1904). Extracts from Joseph Clark can be found in *Red Rubber*.

9. Hochschild, *King Leopold's Ghost*, 271.

10. In three the subject sits in the same chair as Mola Ekulite who was definitely photographed at Ikoko. The other three are identified by Casement as living nearby Bonginda. In neither case is the claim necessarily that the photographs were taken at the mission station. It is merely that they were taken when Casement was staying in that vicinity.

11. This is apparent from Casement's diary of 1903. Renée Mussai, Curator and Head of Archives from Autograph ABF concluded, that 'it seems to me that the montage might be the work of one photographer. Some are duplicates and it appears to be that none of the originals from this montage are represented here in the Harris collection.' (Communication to the writer.)

12. Both Danielsen and Armstrong were present on this occasion as both are witness to this statement. Danielsen's work on this particular slip is covered above, 24. The Belgian government tried to discredit Epondo's statement especially. See Ó Síocháin and O'Sullivan (eds.), *The Eyes*, 36-37, 110–111 and 167–72.

13. Ó Síocháin and O'Sullivan (eds.), *The Eyes*, 108.

14. Ibid., 159–62.

15. Grant, *A Civilised Savagery*, 58.

16. The noteable exception has been Ruth Slade.

17. Alice Seeley Harris is in fact the 'best known missionary photographer; however, she only began' taking atrocity photographs in 1904 (see above, 104). Amongst those historians who have realised this, Armstrong is the most common candidate as photographer. E.g. Grant, *A Civilised Savagery* or Thompson, *Light on Darkness*.

18. Ó Síocháin and O'Sullivan (eds.) *The Eyes*, 304.

19. Morel, *King Leopold's Rule*, 375-377.

20. According to Christina Twomey, Casement's report to Parliament contained no visual images. Christina Twomey, 'Framing Atrocity: Photography and Humanitarianism', *History of Photography*, 36/3 (2012), 255-64, spec. 263.

21. Slivinski has hypothesized that there is only one photographer with reference to two photos: 'The two subjects' poses express striking similarity.' Sharon Sliwinski, '*The Childhood of Human Rights: The Kodak on the Congo*', *Journal of Visual Culture*, vol. 5/3 (December 2006), 334, 338, 340. <http://tps.jkdweb.biz/sites/default/files/uploads/Sliwinski_Kodak_Congo.pdf>, accessed October 2012.

22. For the sake of clarity I note that no one has suggested that Casement took any of these images.

23. University of Edinburgh, Centre for the Study of Christianity in the Non-Western World, Regions Beyond Missionary Union Archive, CSCNWW33, W. D. Armstrong, 'The Earlier Years of the Congo Balolo Mission', unpublished MS.

24. Slade, '*English Missionaries*', 68–9. The initial silence of missionaries to moral outrages in Angola is also noted in Tim Grass, 'Brethren and the Saó Tomé Cocoa Slavery Controversy: The Role of Charles A. Swan (1861–1934)', *Brethren Historical Review*, 4/2 (2007), 110–13.

25. Dugald Campbell to Henry Fox Bourne, 25 July 1905, quoted in Slade, 'English Missionaries', 291–2.

26. Lagergren: *Mission and State in the Congo*, 330.

27. Ibid., 332.

28. Grant, *A Civilised Savagery*, 39.

29. Oral information from the Danielsen family, 2012.

NOTES TO CHAP. 9: PICTURES IN MOTION

1. Thompson, *Light on Darkness*, 229.

2. Ibid., 213.

3. Grant, *A Civilised Savagery*, 60. Grant gives the date as 1903 however there was a one-off lecture in 1903. The tour did not begin till 1904.

4. Thompson, *Light on Darkness*, 213.

5. Grant, *A Civilised Savagery*, 57.

6. The Riley Brothers produced magic lantern shows on important news items of the day. See Pavlakis, *British Humanitarianism* (forthcoming).

7. Thompson, *Light on Darkness*, 232.

8. Grant, *A Civilised Savagery*, 60.

9. *Tingakrossur*, 9 Mar. 1904.

10. Ibid. The earlier article referred to, can be found above in Chap.7, n.10.

11. Thompson, *Light on Darkness*, 194.

12. Cf. EDMP, Morel to Danielson, 17 November, and Morel to Mr. Guinness, copied to Danielson, 16 December 1903, quoted in Jacobsen, *Dollin*, 183–4, 186–7.

13. Morel to Guinness, 17 November 1903.

14. Morel to Danielsen, 17 November 1903.

15. Danielsen arrived back in London before the 16th Oct. This letter is re-published in this volume on page 59.

16. *RB*, Jan.1904; *West African Mail*, 19 Feb. 1904.

17. This is the same boy which Casement's diary seems to suggest of whom Armstrong took a photograph.

18. Photos of Epondo, Ikabo and Epondo, all of which were later incorporated in the Casement Report appear in Morel, *King Leopold's Rule in Africa*, 112.

19. For details on the Belgian accusation of murder on Danielsen's part see page 83. Morel may have also known of the accusations which had been levelled against Danielsen within the CBM. He had heard of Danielsen through James Irvine who sat on the CBM Home Council.

20. Morel, *West Africa*, 334: 'I have in my possession at the present moment a photograph from the Upper Congo of three natives, a woman and two boys; the woman and one of the two boys have their hands severed at the wrist, the other boy has both hands severed.'

21. Morel, *King Leopold's Rule*, 378: 'The correspondent sent me two photographs, one of Mola Ekuliti by himself (which appears in this volume), the other of Mola Ekuliti, in a group of three, a little boy (Mokili) and an old woman (Eyeka).' Morel's correspondent goes on to describe all three as having the same injuries as the figures in the first photograph. Also note that Morel claims that the correspondent sent him the photograph of Mola Ekuliti, when in fact it was part of the group of three early photographs published in *Regions Beyond* and *West African Affairs*. That it was published in the CBM magazine also makes it unlikely to have come from an ABMU correspondent.

22. Ibid., 378-82.

NOTES TO PART 2: MISSIONARY CAMPAIGNS IN THE FAROE ISLANDS

1. Most sections of the 'Brethren' have never adopted a formal name. As a result, they have been variously known as 'Plymouth Brethren', 'Christian Brethren', 'Brethren movement', or simply 'Brethren'. To further complicate matters, they divided in 1848 into 'Open Brethren' and 'Exclusive Brethren'. In the Faroes they were often known as 'Baptists', after their use of believer's baptism by immersion, although sometimes 'Plymouth Brethren' was also used. However, it would appear that W. G. Sloan, following the usage in his native Scotland, explained them to the Faroese as 'Christian Brethren' (*Dimmalætting*, 26 October 1878, quoted in Tórður Jóansson, *Brethren in the Faroes*, 112). Sloan belonged to the Open Brethren, and as Tórður Jóansson in his recent history of the spread of their churches in the Faroes uses the simple term 'Brethren' (Faroese: *Brøður*), this usage is adopted here. For the history of the wider movement in the UK, see Tim Grass, *Gathering to His Name: The Story of Open Brethren in Britain and Ireland* (Milton Keynes, 2006).

2. After 1879 this was known as the Religious Tract and Book Society of Scotland.

3. Fred Kelling, *Fisherman of Faroe: William Gibson Sloan* (Göta, Faroe Islands, 1993).

4. Obituary, *Dimmalætting*, 18 Oct. 1916.

5. Sloan, 'D. J. Danielsen, trúboðari'.

6. Jóanssen, *Brethren in the Faroes*, 43.

7. *Færøsk Kirketidende*, no. 20, 1914.

8. Obituary, *Naade og Sandhed*, No. 11, Nov. 1916.

9. Berghamar: ...*men Gud gav vøkst*, 219–222, 250–254; Kelling, *Fisherman of Faroe*, 182–94; Jóansson, *Brethren in the Faroes*, 158–60.

10. Jóansson, *Brethren in the Faroes*, 161–4.

11. Ibid., 115–17.

12. *EoS* (1905), 105.

13. In fact, he was converted in 1898. This must be either a misprint or a lapse in Danielsen's memory (see above Chap.1, n.9).

14. *EoS* (1905), 184.

15. Jóansson, *Brethren in the Faroes*, 13.

16. *EoS* (1905), 365.

17. *EoS* (1906), 139.

18. Thomas Djonsen (1857–1926) is probably one of the individuals referred to in the letter, cf. Jóansson, *Brethren in the Faroes*, 123.

19. Jóansson, *Brethren in the Faroes*, 13.

20. In Faroese, nouns in the masculine nominative case take the suffix 'ur'; in place names in the letters Danielsen, when it is appropriate (as here), correctly uses the accusative case which as no ending. To avoid confusing English readers, the nominative is used throughout, replacing the accusative in the letters (this follows the practice of Jóansson, *Brethren in the Faroes*).

21. Jóansson, *Brethren in the Faroes*, 120.

22. Ibid., 122.

23. *EoS* (1907), 205–6.

24. Jóansson, *Brethren in the Faroes*, 155–6.

25. Jóansson, *Brethren in the Faroes*, 161.

26. *EoS* (1907), 59.

27. W. T. Stunt *et al., Turning the World Upside Down: A Century of Missionary Endeavour*, 2nd edn (Bath, 1973), 537–8; 'Arthur Charles Gook' <http://en.wikipedia.org/wiki/Arthur_Charles_Gook>, accessed 27 May 2104.

28. Jóansson, *Brethren in the Faroes*, 114.

29. *EoS* (Feb. 1908), 44–5.

30. Jóansson, *Brethren in the Faroes*, 118–19.

31. Ibid., 114.

32. *EoS* (1908), 265.
33. *EoS* (1909), 39.
34. *EoS* (1910), 305.
35. *EoS* (1911), 119.
36. *EoS* (1911), 405.
37. Jóansson, *Brethren in the Faroes*, 120.
38. Ibid., 166–8.
39. *EoS* (May, 1912), 198.
40. Jóansson, *Brethren in the Faroes*, 157–8.
41. Ibid., 25–7, 132, 268–70.
42. Frederick VIII of Denmark had recently died on 14 May 1912. The Order of the Dannebrog is a means of honouring and rewarding the servants of Danish interests for a contribution to the arts, sciences, or business life.
43. *EoS* (1912), 285.
44. *EoS* (1912), 285–6.
45. Jóansson, *Brethren in the Faroes*, 117.
46. *EoS* (1913), 464.
47. It is always possible that these had been inserted by the editors.
48. *EoS* (1913), 347.
49. Kelling, *Fisherman of Faroe*, 232–4.
50. *EoS* (1914), 385.
51. *EoS* (1915), 292.
52. *EoS* (1915), 399.
53. *EoS* (1915), 145–6.
54. Jóansson, *Brethren in the Faroes*, 243.
55. *EoS* (1915), 399.
56. Jóansson, *Brethren in the Faroes*, 166–8.
57. *EoS* (1916), 85–6.
58. CBMM1, 76th Congo Council 28 Feb. 1901.
59. *EoS* (1916), 322.
60. *EoS* (Nov. 1916), 372–3.
61. As has been noted in the text of this section, this was an exaggeration.
62. *EoS* (Nov. 1916), 400.

NOTES TO CONCLUSION

1. The anonymous author of *An Answer to Mark Twain* (Brussels [1907]) was well aware of the sensational nature of the photographs and tried to discredit them. He writes on p.41: 'The Secretary of the Congo Reform Association on present-

ing to the public Mark Twain's soliloquy which he had prompted, knew perfectly well that the soliloquy could not meet with success unless it was illustrated by the usual drawings of alleged acts of cruelty which had promenaded all over England for years in the West African Mail.' He then attempts to discredit the photographs of Epondo, Mola, and Ikabo and dismisses them as being the victim of atrocities inflicted by the authorities.

2. Hochschild, *King Leopold's Ghost*, 271.
3. 'White King, Red Rubber, Black Death (2004)' , YouTube <http://www.you-tube.com/watch?v=aUZLtkLA0VE>, accessed August 2014. There was a repeat broadcast on BBC4 on 14 July 2012.
4. Ruth Slade, *English Missionaries and the Beginning of the Anti-Congolese Campaign in England* (1955), 68–9. The initial silence of missionaries to moral outrages in Angola is also noted by Tim Grass in 'Brethren and the Saó Tomé Cocoa Slavery Controversy: The Role of Charles A. Swan (1861–1934)', *BHR*, 4/2 (2007), 110–13.
5. Lagergren, *Mission and State in the Congo*, 279–80.
6. Neither does Lagergren mention the role of Danielsen in the Congo Campaign whereas he mentions others such as John Harris. That seems to be an unfair omission, especially as Lagergren used Ruth Slade as a source, and she indicates clearly the connection between Danielsen and Morel and the Congo campaign.
7. Dr. Neil Dickson in an e-mail to the writer, 6 Jan. 2014.
8. CBMM1, 26 November 1903.
9. 'The Present Condition of the Congo Free State. – A New Witness', *RB*, Nov. 1903.
10. EDMP, E. D. Morel to D. J Danielsen, 17 November 1903.
11. CBMM1, 26 Nov. 1903.
12. *RB* (1903), 207.
13. Lagergren, *Mission and State in the Congo*, 334, 335.
14. Personal communication, December 2012. Likewise Séamas O Síocháin, Casement's biographer and the editor of his diaries from 1903, wrote 'You have brought Danielson to life and shown his importance.' While Adam Hochschild, the author of *King Leopold's Ghost*, wrote: 'You have done a great job in rescuing this man for history.'

NOTES TO APPENDIX 1

1. Morel, *Red Rubber*, 1.
2. Supplement to *West African Mail*, Sept., 1905.
3. *RB*, Aug.–Sept. 1909; page 142-143.

4. *RB*, Feb. 1910, 24.
5. Ibid.

NOTES TO APPENDIX 2

1. <https://archive.org/details/BokwalaTheStoryOfACongoVictim>, a 304 ccessed 29.7.2014.
2. Note, *RB*, Jan. 1910, 13.
3. *RB* 1905, June, 149.
4. [Lily Ruskin]: *Bokwala. The Story of a Congo Victim* (London, [1909]), 58.
5. Ibid., 69.

BIBLIOGRAPHY

1. Primary Sources
1.1 Manuscript sources

W. D. Armstrong, 'The Earlier Years of the Congo Balolo Mission', unpublished MS, University of Edinburgh, Centre for the Study of Christianity in the Non-Western World, Regions Beyond Missionary Union Archive, CSCNWW33.

Danielsen family papers, A. W. Sloan, 'D. J. Danielsen, trúboðari [missionary] / F. 25. Juni 1871 / D. 18. Oktob. 1916 / Fyrsti føroyski "heidningamissionerur" [The first Faeroese "missionary to the heathen"]', unpublished MS, n.d.

London School of Economics, E. D. Morel papers, MOREL/F1-18.

University of Edinburgh, Centre for the Study of Christianity in the Non-Western World, Regions Beyond Missionary Union Archive, CSCNWW33, CSCN-WW33, Congo Balolo Mission Minutes.

1.2 Newspapers and Journals

Daily Record and Mail [Glasgow newspaper].

Echoes of Service [British Brethren missionary magazine].

Daily Mirror [UK newspaper].

Førøsk Kirkentdende [Faroese established church news].

Tingakrossur [Faroese newspaper].

Naade og Sandhed [periodical published by D. J. Danielsen and Arthur Brend].

Regions Beyond [the periodical of the RBMU].

Vejen [periodical published by Jens av Reyni, Tórshavn, 1941].

West African Mail [the journal of Edmund Morel].

1.2. Printed Primary Sources

Anon: *An Answer to Mark Twain* (Brussels: A. & G. Bulens Bros., [1907]).

Arthur Conan Doyle: *The Crime of Congo* (London: Hutchinson & Co, [1909]).

H. Grattan Guinness: *Congo Slavery: A Brief Survey of the Congo Question from a Humanitarian Point of View* (London: Regions Beyond Missionary Union, 1904).

H. Grattan Guinness: *The Congo Crisis* (London: Regions Beyond Missionary Union, 1908).

H. Grattan Guinness: *"Not unto us:" A Record of Twenty-One Years' Missionary Service* (London, Regions Beyond Missionary Union, 1908).

E. D. Morel: *Affairs of West Africa* (London: Heinemann, 1902).

E. D. Morel: *The Congo Slave State. A Protest against the New African Slavery; and an Appeal to the Public of Great Britain, of the United States, and of the Continent of Europe* (Liverpool: John Richardson & Sons, 1903).

E. D. Morel's History of the Congo Reform Movement (eds.) Wm. Roger Louis and Jean Stengers (Oxford: Clarendon Press, 1968).

E. D. Morel: *King Leopold's Rule in Africa* (London: Heinemann, 1904).

E. D. Morel: *Red Rubber* (London, National Labour Press, 1906).

E. D. Morel: *The Scandal of the Congo: Britain's Duty* (Liverpool: J. Richardson, 1904).

E. D. Morel, *The Treatment of Women and Children in the Congo State. (1895-1904): An Appeal to the Women of the United States of America* (Boston: s.n., 1904).

Syphilia Morgenstierne (ed.): E. D. Morel: *Kongelig Slaveleir* [*Red Rubber* in Norwegian] (Nesbru, Akershus, Norway: Fritt og vilt, 2002).

[Lily Ruskin]: *Bokwala. The Story of a Congo Victim. By a Congo Resident* (London: Religious Tract Society [1909]).

Séamas Ó Síocháin and Michael O'Sullivan (eds.), *The Eyes of Another Race: Roger Casement's Congo Report and 1903 Diary* (Dublin: University College Dublin Press, 2003).

Mark Twain: *King Leopold's Soliloquy: A Defence of His Congo Rule* (Boston: P. R. Warren, 1905).

Henry Wellington Wack: *The Story of the Congo Free State: Social, Political and Economic Aspects of the Belgian System of Government in Central Africa* (New York ; London : G. P. Putnam's Sons, 1905).

2. Secondary Sources

Anti-Slavery International/Autograph: *Republic of the Congo* (London: Autograph ΛBP, [c.2010]).

Sigurd Berghamar: *…men Gud gav vøkst*, (Tórshavn: Afturljóð, 1992).

Joseph F. Conley: *Drumbeats that Changed the World: A History of The Regions Beyond Missionary Union and The West Indies 1873–1999* (Pasadena, CA: World Team International, 2000).

Klaus Fielder: *The Story of Faith Missions: From Hudson Taylor to Present Day Africa* (Carlisle, Cumbria: Regnum, 1994).

Kevin Grant: *A Civilised Savagery: Britain and the New Slaveries in Africa, 1884-1926* (London: Routledge, 2005).

Tim Grass: 'The Development of Support for Overseas Mission in British Assemblies', in Tim Grass (ed.), *Witness in Many Lands: Leadership and Outreach among the Brethren* (Troon, UK: BAHN, 2012), pp.241–62.

Tim Grass: *Gathering to His Name: The Story of the Brethren in Britain and Ireland* (Milton Keynes: Paternoster, 2006).

Tim Grass, 'Brethren and the Saó Tomé Cocoa Slavery Controversy: The Role of Charles A. Swan (1861–1934)', *Brethren Historical Review*, vol. 4 no. 2 (2007), pp.110–13.

John H. Harris: *"Botofé bo le iwa."*: *"Rubber is death" (present day Congo proverb) The Story of the Bongwonga Rubber Collectors* (London: R.B.M.U. Publications Department, 1903).

Adam Hochschild: *King Leopold's Ghost: A Story of Greed, Terror, and Heroism in Colonial Africa* (Boston: Houghton Mifflin Company, 1998).

Óli Jacobsen: *Dollin: Havnarmaðurin sum broytti heimssøguna* (Tórshavn: Forlagið Tjørnustova, 2010).

Óli Jacobsen: 'Daniel J. Danielsen (1871–1916): The Faeroese who Changed History in the Congo', *Brethren Historical Review*, vol. 8 (2012), pp.10–42.

Óli Jacobsen: 'Gamli Sloan 175 ár', *Fríggjadagur*, 9 Aug. 2013, pp.18–19.

Óli Jacobsen: '175 ára føðingardagurin hjá William G. Sloan', *Fríggjadagur*, 27 Sept. 2013, pp.60–1.

Óli Jacobsen: '"Gamli Sloan": William Gibson Sloan after 175 Years', *Brethren Historical Review*, vol. 9 (2013), pp.10–19.

Tórður Jóansson: 'The Brethren in the Faeroes: Some Contexts for Growth', *Brethren Historical Review*, vol. 6 (2010), pp. 54–73.

Tórður Jóansson: *Brethren in the Faroes: An Evangelical Movement, its Remarkable Growth and Lasting Impact in a Remote Island Community* (Tórshavn, 2012).

Fred Kelling: *Fisherman of Faroe: William Gibson Sloan* (Gøta, Faroe Islands: Leirkerið Publications, 1993).

David Lagergren: *Mission and State in the Congo. A Study of the Relations between Protestant Missions and the Congo Independent State Authorities with Special Reference to the Equator District, 1885–1903*, tr. Owen N. Lee (Lund: Gleerup, 1970).

Mac Mckinney, 'Congo', 5-part series, *LA Progressive*, 21 January–5 May 2012.

Síochaín Ó Séamas: *Roger Casement, Imperialist, Rebel, Revolutionary* (Dublin: The Lilliput Press, 2007).

Dean Pavlakis, *British Humanitarianism and the Congo Reform Movement, 1896–1913* (Farnham, Surrey: Ashgate, forthcoming, 2015).

Ruth M. Slade: 'English Missionaries and the Beginning of the Anti-Congolese Campaign in England', *Revue belge de philologie et d'histoire*, vol. 33 No. 1 (1955), pp. 37–73.

Ruth M. Slade: 'English-speaking Missions in the Congo Independent State, 1878-1908', thesis, Bruxelles, 1959.

Sharon Sliwinski, 'The Childhood of Human Rights: The Kodak on the Congo', *Journal of Visual Culture*, 5/3 (December 2006), pp. 333–63.

W. T. Stunt *et al: Turning the World Upside Down: A Century of Missionary Endeavour*, (2nd edn., Bath, Somerset: Echoes of Service, 1973).

T. Jack Thomson: *Light on Darkness? Missionary Photography of Africa in the Nineteenth and Early Twentieth Centuries* (Grand Rapids, MI: Wm. B. Eerdmans Publishing Company, 2012).

David van Reybrouck: *Congo: The Epic History of a People* (2010), Eng. trans. Sam Garrett. (New York: HarperCollins, 2014).

Daniel Vangroenwenge: *Du Sang Sur Les Lianes: Léopold II et son Congo* (Bruxelles: Les Editions Aden, 2010).

John West: *Faroe: The Emergence of a Nation* (London: C. Hurst, 1972).

3. Internet Resources

Africa No. 1 (1904). Correspondence and Report from His Majesty's Consul at Boma Respecting the Independent State of the Congo (London: His Majesty's Stationery Office, 1933) [online text] <https://archive.org/details/CasementReport>.

'Arthur Charles Gook', <http://en.wikipedia.org/wiki/Arthur_Charles_Gook>.

'Bokwala: The Story of a Congo Victim (1910)', Internet Archive <https://archive.org/details/BokwalaTheStoryOfACongoVictim>.

'Congo Balolo Mission', Wikipedia < http://en.wikipedia.org/wiki/Congo-Balolo_Mission>.

'The Brethren Archivists and Historians Network', <http://www.brethrenhistory.org/>.

'Congo Reform Association', Wikipedia <http://en.wikipedia.org/wiki/Congo_Reform_Association>.

Lloyd A. Cooke, 'Terence B. Sawyers' in 'Dictionary of African Christian Biography', <http://www.dacb.org/stories/ghana/sawyers-terence.html> .

'John Hobbis Harris', Wikipedia <http://en.wikipedia.org/wiki/John_Hobbis_Harris>.

Matthew Doherty, 'The Congo Balolo Mission and the Indigenous Christian Community: The Agency of Locals', in Amanda Barry et al. (eds), *Evangelists of Empire?: Missionaries in Colonial History*, [online text] Melbourne: University of

Melbourne Scholarship Research Centre, 2008, <http://msp.esrc.unimelb.edu.au/shs/missions>.

Grove Christian Centre: History', <https://sites.google.com/site/grovechristiancentre/history>.

Marguerite A. Peeters, 'The African Palaver Tradition and the Western Postmodern Consensus: Convergences and Divergences', Dialogue Dynamics, 2009, <http://www.dialoguedynamics.com/content/learning-forum/modules/consensus-palabre/article/the-african-palaver-tradition-and>.

Christina Twomey, 'Framing Atrocity: Photography and Humanitarianism', *History of Photography*, 36/3 (2012), pp.255–64.

<http://tps.jkdweb.biz/sites/default/files/uploads/Sliwinski_Kodak_Congo.pdf>.

White King, Red Rubber, Black Death (2004) , YouTube <http://www.youtube.com/watch?v=aUZLtkLA0VE>.

PHOTO CREDITS

An Answer to Mark Twain, 87

Anti-Slavery International, 46, 62, 63, 100, 104

American Baptist Missionary Union, 43

Neil Dickson, 112

Hervør Djurhuus, FI, 123, 127

Poul Johan Djurhuus, FI, 142

Echoes of Service, 131, 137

Magnus Jacobsen, FI, 17

E. D. Morel, *Affairs of West Africa*, 100

E. D. Morel, *King Leopold's Rule in Africa*, 113, 118

Séamas Ó Síochain: *The Eyes of Another Race*, 20, 44

Kongelig Slavelejr [*Red Rubber* in Norwegian], 54

Naade og Sandhed, FI, 27, 147, 151

Anker Eli Petersen, 95, 154

Regions Beyond, 18, 22, 23, 24, 25, 26, 28, 29, 30, 34, 37, 38, 41, 48, 49, 56, 71, 72, 80, 91, 97, 101, 103, 108, 116, 163, 164, 165, 169

Skandinaver i Congo, Harald Jensen-Tusch, 21

Kári við Rættará, FI, 121, 122

West African Mail, 105

INDEX

Page numbers in **bold** refer to illustrations.

The history of the Congo Reform Movement revised

I published in October 2014 the book *Daniel J. Danielsen and the Congo: Missionary Campaigns and Atrocity Photographs*, which is about an almost unknown Faroese from the North Atlantic, who in 1903 started the lantern lecture campaign, which was the real beginning of the end of King Leopold's rule in the Congo Free State.

When I started my research, there was nearly nothing known about Danielsen's role in the Congo Reform history. In the Faroe Islands I had found only a few sentences indicating, that he was involved in "something" regarding the people of the Congo.

My first main sources were Casement's report and diary and the Morel papers at London School of Economics. Strange enough nothing was found at the RBMU/Balolo Mission archives in Edinburgh. The minute book of the Balolo Mission was quite useful in other questions, but the written material we know that Danielsen brought home from the Congo seems to have disappeared.

In 2010 I published my book about Danielsen's role in the Congo Reform Campaign. It was in Faroese but with a summary in English. I concluded then, that the photos Danielsen brought home from the Congo and used in his campaign had disappeared.

In 2012 Neil Dickson from BAHN, Brethren Archivists & Historian Network, became interested in the history and he asked me to write a summary for their yearly publication, Brethren Historical Review. I looked at the material once again and

and down the Congo River from 17 July to 15 September 1903. Casement wrote later to Foreign Office in London, that Danielsen's *"services were of the very greatest value, indeed without his help I could not have proceeded very far on my journey."*

While coming back to London middle October 1903 Danielsen was eager to convince the Balolo Mission to start a campaign immediately. But the Mission decided to wait for the arrival of Casement 6 weeks later *"before using the information brought home by Mr. Danielson of recent atrocities and ... maladministration of the Congo State"*.

But Danielsen hadn't the patience to wait, and he started his own campaign 7 and 8 November 1903 in Edinburg. When the Balolo mission saw the success of those lectures they started their own campaign already 24 November in Bristol, still before the arrival of Casement. The mission in fact took over Danielsen's campaign.

Furthermore the Foreign Office was aware of Danielsen, and he was intended by them to play a role in the Congo campaign.

This campaign led on 23 March 1904 to the establishment of the Congo Reform Association, whose result was the Belgian annexion of the Congo in 1908.

A question is why Danielsen was completely ignored in the following history writing about the Congo Reform History. We know that Morel and Danielsen had a quite extensive correspondence after Danielsen's arrival from the Congo. But nevertheless Morel didn't even mention him in his books *King Leopold's Rule in Africa, 1904*, and *Red Rubber, 1906*. In the 1950-ies Danielsen was mentioned by Ruth Slade, who

Mission or its historians have never mentioned the role of Danielsen.

One explanation could be Danielsen's temper and lack of patience. It gave him enemies, also among his fellow missionaries. But this characteristic has probably been his strength in the Congo case. He had no patience to wait for the others, and therefore he was ahead of all of them in the Reform Campaign. That is in short the "breaking news" in this history.

Quite a number of authors and historians in North America and Europe have approved my conclusion, even some of them I have corrected. Others have not responded, what I take that they are not able to reject my thesis.

My new book is an updating of my book from 2010. Just before deadline in 2014 I came in contact with Dean Pavlakis, and he got my manuscript. We had a very giving communication, which was of benefit to both of us. We agree that our books are complimentary. Dean's new book, *Humanitarianism and the Congo Reform Movement, 1896-1913*, addresses the bigger questions in Congo Reform history, while my book is especially addressing the history and role of one actor, D. J. Danielsen. These books are together the closest to the truth about the Congo Reform Movement it is possible to come with the available sources.

The book will be available at the symposium free of charge. It can be read on www.olijacobsen.com. My e-mail is: olijacobsen@olivant.fo

These sources indicated that Casement brought those photos to England. But as he arrived to London 1 December 1903 and the lantern lectures started in November, there was obviously a different explanation for the photos.

These photos were by some sources, also Morel, attributed to the Balolo Mission missionary William D. Armstrong, working in Bonginda together with Danielsen. But Casement's diary only mentions one photo taken by Armstrong. But according to the date the photo was taken it was certainly not used in the campaign.

The first photos used in the campaign were taken in two different places, Ikoko and Bonginda, likely by the same photographer. As only Danielsen had been in both places, the photographer could not be Armstrong. It was most likely Danielsen.

It is almost official history in England is that those first photos derive from Alice Harris. That is certainly wrong, as her first known atrocity photo is from 14 May 1904, half a year after Danielsen's start of his lantern campaign in November 1903.

Furthermore the Harris's were not the first in the Congo Lantern Campaign. They joined the already running campaign in October 1905. It is likely that Harris's as others were inspired by the success of the campaign started by Danielsen. The Harris's did certainly a great job for the Congo case, but that was after Danielsen.

Danielsen's first effort was as the assistant of Casement on the boat "Henry Red" up

The Congo Balolo Mission.

Advisory Council.

THE DIRECTORS OF THE R.B.M.U.
P. S. BADENOCH, ESQ.
H. B. BILBROUGH, ESQ.
RICHARD CORY, ESQ., J.P.
W. MCADAM ECCLES, ESQ., M.S., F.R.C.S.
MRS. H. GRATTAN GUINNESS.

THE REV. D. HAYES.
G. E. HOLMAN, ESQ.
JAMES IRVINE, ESQ., F.R.G.S.
PRINCIPAL FORBES JACKSON, M.A.
THE REV. A. J. PALMER.
J. CHRISTIE REID, ESQ.

Seventeen years have passed since the **CONGO BALOLO MISSION** began to evangelize the millions of Balolo peoples inhabiting the horse-shoe bend of the Congo. During that time it has accomplished a large amount of pioneer work, and established six Stations. **LEOPOLDVILLE**, about 360 miles from the coast, is the business base of the Mission, and an encouraging Evangelistic work is in progress there. At **LOLANGA**, on the Upper River, more than 800 miles inland, the members of the native church are conspicuous for the zeal with which they seek to carry the Gospel into the regions beyond—those surrounding towns and villages which have never yet heard of **JESU'S** Name. **LOLANGA**, is also the headquarters of the Building Department, a most necessary adjunct to a Central African Mission.

The four remaining stations, situated on tributaries of the Congo, are still further inland. The **TWO MISSION STEAMERS**, the "Pioneer" and the "Livingstone," find their home at **BONGINDA**, with the result that the missionaries there are chiefly engaged in evangelizing and teaching a large staff of native workmen who, with their wives and families, make up the chief part of the population. Itinerating work is also carried on from this station, and from **IKAU**, another centre where C. B. M. missionaries have long ministered to the people. The **PRINTING PRESS** of the Mission is established at **BONGANDANGA**, and its native staff is now printing the **NEW TESTAMENT IN LOMONGO**, from a translation made by C. B. M. workers. The "**CONGO BALOLO MISSION RECORD**" is also published there quarterly,

THE CONGO BALOLO MISSION RECORD.

3rd. Year.   1907.   3rd. Quarter.

Contents.

	PAGE
COME YE APART	25
ANSWERED PRAYER AT IKAU	26
TO REACH THE GIRLS AT BONGINDA	27
The work at Baringa.	
ON THE STATION	29
THE VOICE OF THE BEYOND	30
JEHOVAH JESUS	32
Missionary Life.	
AN HOUR IN TOWN	33
A DAY IN THE LIFE OF AN ARTISAN MISSIONARY	35
The Children's Corner.	
A PEEP AT CONGO CHILDREN	Cover.
C. B. M. CENTRES AND MISSIONARIES	Cover.

Congo Balolo Mission.
Congo Independent State.

Edited and Printed
at Bongandanga
Central Africa.

and sent direct to its English subscribers for 1s. per annum, or specimen copies are supplied from Harley House. It contains most interesting contributions from the various Missionaries, and gives some idea of the intensity of the struggle in which they are engaged. Baringa, the sixth C.B.M. station, is situated more than 1,100 miles from the coast, and has been the scene of some of the worst atrocities connected with the iniquitous rubber traffic. But notwithstanding the intolerable cruelties from which the Congolese suffer, their deepest need is the need of salvation and cleansing from sin, and in the great task of ministering to that need more than forty C.B.M. missionaries are at work in the field. Many more helpers are needed, and funds for extension are urgently required. Since the Mission was started, more than **ONE HUNDRED MEN AND WOMEN** have been sent out, and of these forty-one have surrendered their lives in the work. They rest from their labours, but the fruit of their efforts is seen in the increasing love of the people for those who prove to be their best friends. Tribes that once indulged in cannibal practices are now asking for teachers; the Gospels are eagerly read in the native tongue, and in the midst of their darkness, these cruelly oppressed peoples are learning that GOD is Light.

Any who would like to help in this work for the sake of the Kingdom should apply to its Acting Director,

H. GRATTAN GUINNESS, M.D.,
Harley House, Bow, London, E.